THE BRI
BLI'

**Danger UXB. An unexploded bomb dropped on
the town centre on December 11, 1940.**

David Rowland

S. B. Publications

THIS book is dedicated to the civilian men, women and children who were killed in Brighton as a result of enemy action between 1940 and 1944.

First published in 1997 by S. B. Publications,
c/o 19 Grove Road, Seaford, East Sussex BN25 1TP

ISBN 1 85770 124 0

Designed and typeset by CGB, Lewes
Printed by Island Press Ltd
3 Cradle Hill Industrial Estate, Seaford, East Sussex BN25 3JE
Tel: 01323 490222

CONTENTS

Cover pictures:
Front: A householder looks at the Morrison shelter which saved the lives of his wife and his son when their home collapsed around them.
Back: Railway lines hang in the air after a bomb which travelled through the corner house exploded on the viaduct.

ACKNOWLEDGEMENTS

I wish to record my thanks to those wonderful people who gave me their time and offered their reminiscences – often painful reminders of terrible times.

Thank you, too, to those who wrote to me in response to a number of requests in the local press; to the publisher who, like I do, believes the content of this book is part of the history of Brighton and should be available to all who wish to learn about how it suffered in, and survived the Second World War; and to my wife, Christine, who has had to live with this project for the past six years.

PICTURE CREDITS

The author is grateful to John Grinstead, Mrs Dulcie Wisdom and Mrs Peggy Lower for permission to use photographs from their personal collections; to Brighton Reference Library for material from its newspaper archives; to the Public Record Office, Kew, for photographs on pages 53, 61, 65, 66, 67 and the back cover also to the *Evening Argus;* to the *Brighton Herald,* publishers of *Brighton in Battledress;* and to the Southern Publishing Company, publishers of *Brighton and Hove Under Fire.*

BIBLIOGRAPHY

Brighton and Hove Herald
Brighton Evening Argus
Brighton in Battledress by D L Murray, *Brighton Herald*, 1946
Brighton and Hove Under Fire, compiled Leslie G Cluett, Southern Publishing Company 1946
Public Record Office, Kew

INTRODUCTION

OVER many years I have told the story of the time a German aircraft machine-gunned the road I was in as I walked home from school for lunch. The truth of this tale was questioned by one or two people and so I set out to prove that it actually happened. Naively, I thought that 'my' incident was the only time that the streets of Brighton were machine-gunned.

I had been walking home from Finsbury Road School in Southover Street with a friend. At the junction of Grove Street and Albion Hill I saw an aircraft coming across town from the direction of the railway station. It was very low and we both realised that it was a German plane. We ran for shelter in the archway of Chates Farm in Albion Hill. As we reached the archway the plane's guns opened up and fired all the way up the hill. All this happened in seconds.

Although I knew roughly the time, I did not know the date and so that is what I set out to discover. I started to make a list of the dates of the raids on Brighton; this took an enormous amount of time as the official records have been lost over the years. Eventually I found out that the first air raid was in July 1940, but that was all I knew.

A couple of good friends, Bob Elliston and George Humphrey, gave me some very good advice and pointed me in the right direction – just as well as I was about to forget the whole idea. Another good friend, Lionel Quinlan, also helped and encouraged me. But then I started to hit a number of snags; there were now no official records at the hospitals, the police station or the fire station, and only limited information was available in the Brighton reference library.

Once again I started to lose interest in the project – but then I had a couple of letters in the *Evening Argus* that brought some interesting replies and these gave me fresh inspiration.

I moved my research to London and before long started to find the information I was seeking. By this time close on five years had elapsed and eventually I discovered that the day I had remembered all these years, when a German aircraft came towards me across town, with guns blazing, was Tuesday, May 25, 1943. I was seven years old.

Originally, the book was intended as an account of that raid, generally accepted as one of the worst suffered by Brighton, but by this time I had amassed a great deal of information about the bombing of Brighton and the book has grown to become a record of many of the air attacks on the town.

David Rowland,
Telscombe Cliffs, 1996

1

FIERCE FIRES AND GREAT EXPLOSIONS

BETWEEN Monday, July 15 1940 and Wednesday, March 22, 1944, Brighton suffered fifty six air attacks, during which 381 high explosive bombs and many hundreds of incendiary bombs were dropped. In all 198 people lost their lives, 357 were seriously injured and another 433 were slightly injured.

Some 200 houses were completely demolished, 894 were badly damaged and 14,232 received slight damage.

These official figures cannot convey the terror, heartache and anguish experienced by those who lived through the war years. Brighton was not among the worst bombed towns in England, but few suffered such a protracted period of attack. Why was this, when the area had no obvious military targets? The reason later became apparent when German records showed that Sussex to the east of Brighton was designated by Hitler as one of the main invasion areas, and the continual air attacks may have been a softening up process.

Also, many German pilots, driven from their targets inland by the strength of air and coastal defences – especially during the Battle of Britain and the London Blitz – jettisoned their bombs over the coast and seaside towns and turned tail.

Others, on reconnaissance missions, or hunting for shipping, would swoop on the seaside towns – a comparatively safe and easy way of providing reports of 'fierce fires and great explosions'.

Then there were the tip and run raids launched from airfields little more than sixty miles away on the French coast. German aircraft crossed the Channel, dropped their bombs on 'easy' targets and fled back across the water. The object was to terrorise the inhabitants.

Three raids in particular stand out in Brightonians' memories: the day the Odeon Cinema in Kemp Town was bombed on September 14,

**Barbed wire and an anti aircraft gun on Marine Parade, near Paston Place and,
below, beach defence works and the Palace Pier with its central span demolished
as a precaution against invasion.**

1940, when fifty two people died; the day the children's clinic was bombed on March 23, 1943, when nineteen people were killed, including one of the German pilots; and the worst raid of the war, May 25, 1943, 'the day the bomb bounced through a house in Argyle Villas and demolished the viaduct', and twenty four people died.

Another tragedy that stays in people's minds is the scandal of the mother and four children trapped under the rubble of their bombed house for fifty six hours while members of the rescue service clocked off at 7pm when daylight still remained, and clocked on again at 7am the next morning.

East Brighton bore the brunt of the bombing and Marine Gate, the block of flats at Black Rock, was the most heavily attacked building in the town. Obviously it had no military significance, but it was very tall, very white and an easy target for raiders coming in across the Channel. The block was bombed repeatedly, strafed with machine gun fire and suffered further damage from the massive explosions when the nearby gas holders went up. Yet the battle scarred building was still standing when the war ended, still occupied by its indefatigable residents.

At the outbreak of war Brighton's famous beaches were made off-limits, pleasure craft and fishing boats were removed to Sheepcote Valley and the pond in Queen's Park, and both piers were severed in the middle to prevent their use by invaders coming in from the sea.

2

THE FIRST ATTACKS

MONDAY, JULY 15, 1940.

IT was a dismal, damp morning and early workers were already up and about, delivering post and milk, sweeping the streets, emptying the dustbins when Brighton suffered its first raid.

Just before 6am the drone of a single aircraft was heard. Few, looking up, would have recognised the Dornier DO17. A couple of minutes later bombs were dropping – described by witnesses as screaming and whistling down. They landed on houses in Whitehawk Road, Princes Terrace and Bristol Gardens, killing four people and seriously injuring

Whitehawk Road pictured on the morning of Monday, July 15, 1940.
Photo: Evening Argus

another five. Eleven others were less seriously hurt and were treated at the scene by local first aiders.

Ettie Hargreaves, a woman of sixty seven, was the first Brighton person to be killed by a bomb; she died in her home in Princes Terrace. James Sawyer, seriously injured outside the Clyde Arms, Bristol Gardens, died the following day in hospital; George Wood, from Maresfield Road, died two days later in hospital; and the third victim, Henry May, father of six children, suffered horrific injuries and died in the ambulance taking him to hospital.

Newspaper reporters were quickly on the scene and in the *Brighton Herald* an ARP warden was quoted as saying that the spirit of the people was high. One group of children had met him with smiles, he said, and were quite cheerful even though a bomb had fallen in their garden. He called at another house and was greeted by a man who said: 'Today is my seventy fourth birthday; this is a nice present from Hitler!' Then he and his wife set about getting cups of tea for the rescue workers – who had reached the scene within twenty minutes.

By 10.30am as many as eighteen firms of builders were at work clearing debris, filling craters in the road and making houses safe from collapse.

KILLED BY ENEMY ACTION ON MONDAY JULY 15 1940

HARGREAVES Ettie, 67, 13 Princes Terrace.
MAY Henry, 35, 64 Manor Hill.
SAWYER (Francis) James, 43, 11 Manor Road, in the Royal Sussex County Hospital the following day.
WOOD George, 52, 9 Maresfield Road, two days later in the Royal Sussex County Hospital.

Flames 100ft high destroyed the roof and top floor of the Intermediate School in York Place.

SUNDAY AUGUST 25 1940

AT about 10.05pm on that summer Sunday night a number of German aircraft flew low over Brighton dropping incendiary bombs as well as machine-gunning the town centre. The air raid sirens had sounded their warning only as the planes appeared overhead and there was little time to find shelter. Those still about threw themselves under parked vehicles and rushed for the relative safety of doorways.

Fires started all over town, the most serious at the Intermediate School in York Place where flames roared 100 feet into the sky and the inferno burned for many hours before it was finally brought under control. The roof and top floor of the school were severely damaged.

Another fire destroyed Eede and Butt's timber yard in Trafalgar Lane and incendiaries also started a huge fire at Tamplins Brewery's wine store behind Richmond Terrace. Large stocks of champagne and wine were lost as the store was gutted, and considerable damage was caused to a building where the brewery's packing materials were stored. Tamplins' manager had high praise for the firemen whose 'tireless work' prevented total loss of the buildings.

The flames from these and other, smaller, fires lit up the town centre, making it appear as if the whole of Brighton were on fire. The situation was so dangerous that police evacuated residents from a large part of the area. The *Brighton Herald* reported that: 'The local population, although some had been subjected to machine gun fire, took the situation very calmly and it would seem indeed that the determination for complete victory at all costs was strengthened in these people whose homes were suddenly put in peril'.

The scene inside the Odeon Cinema where twelve people were killed or died later from their injuries.

In the same raid homes in Upper Bedford Street were smashed to matchwood.

3

THE DAY THEY HIT
THE ODEON

SATURDAY SEPTEMBER 14 1940

THE bombing of Brighton on this Saturday afternoon became known as 'Brighton's worst air raid' or 'the day they hit the Odeon'. Whether it was the worst is debatable; what is certain is that there was extensive damage and terrible loss of life.

At about 3.40pm a German bomber, possibly a Dornier DO17, was seen being hotly pursued by a Spitfire over Brighton. The chase started to the east of the town and, over Kemp Town, in an effort to get away, the raider released its bomb load. It was reported at the time that seven bombs were dropped, but only six have been traced.

They exploded almost simultaneously and within just a few minutes of absolute terror fifty two people lost their lives, another eighty five suffered horrific injuries and many others were less seriously hurt.

The bombs fell in an east-west line on Kemp Town Place, the Odeon Cinema in St George's Road, Upper Bedford Street, Hereford Street, Upper Rock Gardens and Edward Street.

The main rescue efforts were concentrated on the cinema where about 300 people had been watching the film. It was seen as a miracle that more people were not killed. The bomb scored a direct hit on the Odeon, crashing through the roof and exploding in the north eastern corner, close to the screen. Two children and two adults were killed outright and another ten suffered such severe injuries that they died later that same day at the Royal Sussex County Hospital.

The film was a comedy, *The Ghost Comes Home*, starring Frank Morgan, Billie Burke and Ann Rutherford. It had started at 3.30pm. Some newspaper reports of the time, perhaps wanting to add to the drama of their accounts, named the film as *It Could Happen To You*. This was, in fact, the other half of a double bill and had already finished.

Passers by and workers from Kemp Town Brewery (including the author's father, Charles, and his friend, Bob Hunt) beat the rescue services to the scene and plunged into the wrecked cinema to help people out and look after the many terrified children.

Initially there was utter confusion with injured and frightened people everywhere. Some of the small shops in St George's Road, opposite the cinema, had suffered severe blast damage and shop workers tumbled out into the street, dazed and injured, with blood and dust covering their faces. Some just sat down on the kerb, while others sank to their knees, thankful to be alive.

Because the chased bomber had appeared so quickly there had been no time to sound the alarm, no time for people to take to the shelters.

Ambulances and requisitioned vehicles ferried the injured and dying to the nearby hospital and doctors and nurses rushed to the cinema to give what help they could.

Bridget Groves, then Bridie Hassett, one of ten children living at Manor Farm, remembers the Odeon bombing as a personal nightmare for her family. Her brother Jack had gone to the matinee at the Odeon with his friends and her mother was frantic – until Jack turned up alive and well much later, having gone to another cinema instead.

Bridie recalled: 'I can still see the processions of little coffins going down our street all that following week, the older folk sobbing. I can remember that I felt rather strange that I would never see my best friend Mary Sharpe again.'

Tony Bishop has traumatic memories of that dreadful day. He was nine years old at the time and lived with his parents, and sister Connie, fourteen, in Fletching Road, Whitehawk. His father was serving with the 13th/18th Royal Hussars and his mother worked as a cleaner at Brighton General Hospital.

Tony and Connie asked if they could go to the pictures as their mother would be at work from 2pm to 10pm, but she said they were not to. No sooner had Mrs Bishop left for work than Tony and Connie put on their best clothes and headed for the Odeon.

He recalls: 'I remember there was a good audience. We sat in the middle block of seats on the ground floor, near to the left side gangway. In the seat in front of me was a soldier. The film was at a point where a door opened and a hand and forearm appeared; the hand was about to grab hold of a bottle of milk on a shelf near the door when there was a terrifying rattle, almost like a shower of giant hailstones landing on the roof of the cinema. In a split second the rattle was followed by an enormous explosion and I saw the soldier in front of me had no head.

'Within that same time, which seemed to last for ages, there was a blinding flash. I tried to hide under my seat, as we had been taught to do at school, but my seat seemed to have disappeared.

'My next recollection was of sunlight streaming down from the roof area. I remember noticing that dust was swirling about in clouds and streamers, and I could hear people screaming and calling for help. I stood up and started to climb over the debris to get to the exit and foyer of the cinema. I moved a few yards and then something fell and hit me on the head and stunned me. I came round quickly and could still hear screams and cries for help.

'The exit was nearby and I went out at the east side of the foyer, where I then fainted. I came to and saw people coming into the cinema from St George's Road to help those inside. At that point I made my own way out into St George's Road. Paston Place was a few steps away and I knew that I was hurt, so I started to walk up Paston Place towards the Sussex County Hospital at the top of the street. A few yards up the street I fainted again and when I came to a postman, a Mr White, who lived in Sudeley Street, was carrying me to the hospital. He took me to the outpatients building which was opposite the main Eastern Road entrance to the hospital. In the building I was laid on the floor. On one side of me was a man who had had an arm blown off. He died. On the other side was a woman who had had her leg blown off. She also died.

'A doctor examined me and a nurse took small fragments of shrapnel from my chest, where they had lodged under the skin. They stitched a wound in my thorax – no anaesthetic – and then I can remember being taken home to Whitehawk by an air raid warden – on a normal service bus!'

When he reached his home a neighbour took Tony in and he was put to bed in her house. The neighbour contacted Mrs Bishop who rushed home. Connie, meanwhile, had reached home unaided and had a small shrapnel wound in her knee. Both children had lost most of their hair on one side of the head. What really upset Tony was that he had shrapnel holes in his best top coat, pullover, shirt and vest, and he feared his mother's wrath.

But the boy's ordeal was not over. Later that night, in shock and having difficulty breathing, he was seen by a doctor and taken by police car to Brighton General where he was found to have small pieces of shrapnel in his diaphragm. Some were removed, but one piece was left in situ and remains with him to this day. He was in hospital for four weeks and during that time there was a dog fight when two planes flew past the hospital at roof level, firing their guns. 'It was dinner time and my plate was on a tray on my lap in bed,' Tony remembers. 'I threw my tray up in the air and I was under the bed before it hit the floor.'

He says: 'There was no counselling available at that period of our history. I do have a certificate somewhere, recording that I was injured, but feel it would be inappropriate to try to claim compensation!'

Connie escaped death again when, later, she was due on fire watching night duty at St Cuthman's Church in Whitehawk. She swapped the duty and later that night a bomb scored a direct hit on the church, killing the warden on duty.

Meanwhile, the enemy aircraft that had caused such devastation and carnage in the cinema, had bombed Kemp Town Place, flattening number 8, where three members of the Rush family were killed – Alan, an ARP ambulance driver and two of his daughters, Margaret, seventeen, and Yvonne just eleven months old.

Josephine Claney, of 8a Kemp Town Place, was severely injured and died later that day in hospital.

Another of the bombs hit 36 and 37 Upper Bedford Street, and yet another fell some yards away in Hereford Street. Number 36 Upper Bedford Street was Mitchell's, a grocery, and 37 was a general store known as Clapham's. These two shops were between Manchester Row and Crescent Cottages. The blast from the bomb took out the shops and houses on the opposite side of the street and properties on either side of the bombed shops were severely damaged.

Two children were playing in Hereford Street when the bombs fell. They were among the fifty two victims of the raid.

The story was very similar in Hereford Street. Iris Chapman, a fourteen year old girl riding her bicycle along the street, and ten year old George Bailey, playing on the street corner, were both killed. As the afternoon unfolded the death toll mounted. In total fourteen people lost their lives in this area, their ages ranging from ten to thirty eight. Many of the injured just sat quietly on the pavements, too dazed to do anything but stare in utter disbelief at the scene around them.

One of the string of bombs hit two large three storey houses in Upper Rock Gardens. Numbers 30 and 31 were at the top of the road at the junction with Edward Street. Buried under tons of debris, six people died – Julia Duran, Susannah Everett and her nine year old daughter Monica, Charles and Charlotte Burkinshaw and Lena Varney.

Just a few hundred yards down the road in Edward Street the sixth bomb caused damage to the premises of Braybon's, the builders, and killed David Jones whose home at 30 Upper Rock Gardens had been demolished seconds earlier.

The rescue services worked through the night, by the inadequate light of shaded torches, in an effort to save people still trapped in the cinema ruins, and under the debris of their homes.

KILLED AS A RESULT OF ENEMY ACTION ON SATURDAY SEPTEMBER 14 1940

ALLWRIGHT Robert William, 14, 18 Somerset Street, injured in Bedford Street, died the same day at RSCH.

BAILEY George, 10, 18 Upper Bedford Street, died at the corner of Hereford Street.

BALDWIN Stanley, 14, ARP messenger, 93 Twineham Road, Whitehawk, injured at the Odeon, died the same day at RSCH.

BALL Frederick, 57, Air Raid Warden, 4 Clarendon Terrace, injured at Chesham Place and died same day at RSCH.

BARTON Edith Emily, 62, 137 Whitehawk Crescent, at the Odeon.

BLACKWELL Jane, 67, 10 Sussex Square, injured in Kemp Town and died the following day at RSCH.

BORROW Sidney Roy, 11, 113 Maresfield Road, Manor Farm, injured at Odeon Cinema and died later the same day at RSCH.

BRASHILL Lilian May, 22, 33 Hodshrove Road, Moulescombe, at 34 Hereford Street.

BROWN Edward Clark, 10, 28 Somerset Street, at Hereford Street.

BURKINSHAW Charles, 69, 31 Upper Rock Gardens.

BURKINSHAW Charlotte, 69, 31 Upper Rock Gardens.

CHAPMAN Alfred, 18, 36 Hervey Road, Whitehawk, injured at the Odeon Cinema, died same day at RSCH.

CHAPMAN Iris Lilian, 14, 30 Upper Bedford Street, at Hereford Street.

CLANCY Josephine Trissie, 36, 8a Kemp Town Place, taken to RSCH and died the same day.

CORDIER Joan May, 16, 66 Queens Park Rise, at 36 Upper Bedford Street.

DAVIES Ivor David, 14, 108 Hervey Road, Whitehawk, injured at the Odeon Cinema and died the following day at RSCH.

DUPLOCK Monica Mary Ann, 9, 49 Whitehawk Avenue, at RSCH.

DURAN Julia, 73, 49 Oxford Road, Kilburn, at 30 Upper Rock Gardens.

EVERETT Monica, 9, 30 Upper Rock Gardens.

EVERETT Susannah Mary, 34, 30 Upper Rock Gardens.

HARRIS Freda, 14, 26 Freshfield Street, injured at Odeon Cinema, died same day at RSCH.

INMAN Nora, 52, 153 Holbein House, Holbein Place, London, died the following day at RSCH.

JONES David Thomas, 31, 30 Upper Rock Gardens, at Braybons in Edward Street.

JONES Leonard Henry, 59, 24 Sussex Square, injured in St George's Road, died same day at RSCH.

LEECH Louisa Kate Maud, 60, 4 Chichester Place.
LOFTUS Nellie Irene, 15, 42 Manor Hill, Manor Farm, injured at Odeon Cinema and died same day at RSCH.
MACDONALD Joseph Hilton Salvage, 38, 2 Hereford Street.
MARCHANT Johanna, 55, 4 Manor Hill, Manor Farm, at the Odeon Cinema.
MARTIN Harry, 18, 19 Upper Bedford Street, at 14 Upper Bedford Street (Mephams, pork butchers).
MASKELL Charles Hackney, 67, 7 Rock Grove, at Chesham Road.
MASON Edith Ellen, 68, 15a Eaton Place, injured at Odeon, died on November 18 at RSCH.
MEPHAM Arthur, 30, 11 Peel Road, at 14 Upper Bedford Street (Mephams).
MITCHELL Bertha Matilda, 38, 36 Upper Bedford Street.
RENNIE Elizabeth Ann, 67, 3 St George's Terrace, at 35 Upper Bedford Street (Howells, fishmongers).
RICHARDSON Alice, 30, 34 Hereford Street.
RICHARDSON George Noel, 11, 34 Hereford Street.
SHARPE Mary Elizabeth, 11, 24 Manor Way, injured at Odeon and died same day at RSCH.
ROGERS Violet, 17, 13 Blaker Street, at Bedford Street.
ROSENZWEIG Lilian Jean, 46, 34 Camelford Street, injured at Odeon, died same day at RSCH.
RUSH Alan James, 52, 8 Kemp Town Place.
RUSH Margaret Lilian, 17, 8 Kemp Town Place, injured at home and died same day at RSCH.
RUSH Yvonne, 11 months, 8 Kemp Town Place, injured at home and died same day at RSCH.
STURGESS Pamela Violet, 6, 2 Riflebutt Road, at Odeon Cinema.
STUTTERFORD Frank Peter Hugo, 15, Portland Place, on duty for St John Ambulance Brigade at Odeon.
SWAIN Herbert, 43, 12a Canon Place, at Eaton Place.
THOMAS Joyce Alma, 17, 14 Pankhurst Avenue, at 15 Upper Bedford Street (newsagents).
VARNEY Lena, 29, 31 Upper Rock Gardens.
WALKER Ronald William Noah Swift, 40, 5 West Hill Street, injured at Odeon Cinema and died same day at RSCH.
WARNETT Ellen Mary, 41, 69 Whitehawk Road, at RSCH.
WOOD Mary Marjorie, 25, 22 St George's Terrace, at Hereford Street.
WOOD Ronald, 11 months, 22 St George's Terrace, at Hereford Street.
WRIGHT Maria, 70, 4 Hereford Street, injured at home and died following day at Brighton General Hospital (BGH).

This iron bedstead and wardrobe are all that remain of a first floor bedroom in one of the houses in White Street.

WEDNESDAY SEPTEMBER 18 1940

THE sirens had already sounded and the pips, indicating a raid was imminent, were still being heard when a lone German fighter-bomber appeared and dived low, dropping bombs in the Edward Street area. It was 8.17pm.

A direct hit on the houses towards the bottom part of White Street reduced them to a heap of rubble and caused a large crater in the road. Eleven people in the four houses were killed, including a family of five, and a twelfth person died in Blaker Street, in a house backing on to the bombed homes.

The explosion was heard over a large area and serious damage was caused to nearby properties with the roads and gardens littered with thousands or roof slates and tiles, and glass from shattered windows.

Pieces of debris were flung long distances; the wheels of a mangle ended up embedded in a roof in the next street. A second bomb fell on a builder's yard in Mighell Street and a heavy iron girder, twelve feet long and weighing two hundredweight, was hurled over a house roof in White Street, a distance of about seventy five yards. From the same yard, the iron wheel from a wheelbarrow was flung over roof tops and was found more than 300 yards away.

In a nearby street a policeman picked up a book that had been thrown through the air – it was called *All Quiet on The Western Front*.

Emergency workers were soon on the scene to rescue victims in the bombed and damaged houses and to evacuate neighbours from unsafe buildings. Streets were roped off, guards were posted and a fleet of ambulances took the injured to hospital.

Those made homeless were sheltered in local public halls where, in many instances, they joined victims of the previous Saturday's attack when the Odeon Cinema was bombed.

Rescuers worked in the debris at great personal risk because of the perilous condition of the bombed houses, carrying on the search for victims throughout the night.

**KILLED AS A RESULT OF ENEMY ACTION
ON WEDNESDAY SEPTEMBER 18 1940**

COATMAN Elizabeth, 78, 5 White Street
COTMAN Henry Joel, 84, 5 White Street, at BGH on October 8
FREEMAN Agnes Florence Mary, 60, 4 White Street, two days later at RSCH.
NORRIS Jane Maria, 70, 2 White Street.
O'CONNELL Eileen Florence, 20, 2 White Street
O'CONNELL Eileen Mary, nine months, 2 White Street.
PERRY Joan Constance, 22, 4 Acton Lane, Harlesdon, Middlesex (daughter of Ernest Tucker) at 6 White Street.
PERRY Rita Joan, nine months, 4 Acton Lane, Harlesdon, Middlesex.
TUCKER Albert Edward, 27, 6 White Street.
TUCKER Edward Ernest, 55, 6 White Street
TUCKER Maude Charlotte Mary, 6 White Street.
WICKENS Julia Emily, 72, 5 Blaker Street.

The Franklin Arms in Lewes Road after a lone Junkers 88 jettisoned its bombs.
Below: Rescuers search the wreckage. After three hours they located and
released barmaid Betty Marchant.

5

LONE RAIDERS AND INCENDIARY ATTACKS

FRIDAY SEPTEMBER 20 1940

CLOSE to midday on this autumn Friday wailing sirens warned of an impending air attack. Almost immediately the drone of aircraft engines was heard. People scattered from the streets, searching for any type of shelter. Then, suddenly, bombs were falling from a low flying, unidentified plane. It was later reported that a Junkers 88, returning from a bombing mission over south east England, was attacked by RAF fighters and failed to return to its base in France.

One bomb almost completely destroyed the Franklin Arms, a large pub at 158 Lewes Road, close to the junction with Franklin Road. It was later rebuilt and named the Lewes Road Inn. In the same raid, three small terraced houses in Caledonian Road were razed to the ground and extensive damage was caused to other property and several shops.

People living and working in the area spoke later of the amount of black coal dust, and the feathers – from the feather mattresses then popular – that hung in the air in the wake of the raid.

When rescue workers arrived passers-by were already tearing at the rubble with their bare hands. Fifteen people lost their lives in this raid, including a one month old girl, and many suffered serious injuries.

One of the most dramatic rescues was at the pub. Civil defence workers and soldiers searched for nearly two hours before barmaid Betty Marchant was located. She was conscious, but trapped beneath tons of fallen masonry. Betty had been serving behind the bar when the bomb dropped and as she fell to the floor the bar had collapsed over her – but had also protected her from falling debris. Eventually, three hours after the disaster, Betty was brought out pale and weak. When a friend called out to her she responded with a faint wave.

Meanwhile the work went on in an effort to rescue others trapped in the ruins of the pub. The water main had been fractured and water was flowing into the cellars, hampering the rescuers. They then managed to locate the licensee, Ernest Sully, who was conscious but badly injured. Frantic efforts were made to free him but when eventually he was released from the wreck of his pub he was dead. Shortly afterwards the body of his wife Rosina was found.

KILLED AS A RESULT OF ENEMY ACTION ON FRIDAY SEPTEMBER 20 1940

BOYLING Arthur George, 35, 23 Hampstead Road, at 159B Lewes Road.

DANNIGAN Alma Madeline, 26, 55 Southover Street, in St Leonard's Road.

GLYDE Emily, 57, 21 Caledonian Road.

HOOK Ann Terase, 1 month, 42 Dudley Road, in Caledonian Road.

HOOK Edith May Kathleen, 26, 42 Dudley Road, in Caledonian Road.

MORLEY Arthur, 62, 22 Caledonian Road.

MORLEY Mabel Frances, 60, 22 Caledonian Road.

PULLEN Violet Louise, 36, 9 St Mary Magdalene Street, at Lewes Road Inn.

RIDOUT Freda Mary, 25, 16 Bernard Road, in Upper Lewes Road.

SAYERS Elizabeth Lydia, 88, 22 Caledonian Road, at 17 Caledonian Road.

SINDEN Jane, 87, 21 Caledonian Road.

TOOTELL Emma, 77, 20 Shaftesbury Road, injured in Lewes Road, died same day at BGH.

WATSON John, 56, 115 Bear Road, who was cleaning the pub windows.

WELLS George, 65, 72 Franklin Road.

WELLS Sydney George, 68, 7 Dinapore Street, injured at home, died BGH October 23.

TUESDAY SEPTEMBER 24 1940

IT was a little after 3.30pm and children, just out of school, were playing happily in the streets in and around Albion Hill when the sound of a low flying aircraft was heard. No sirens were sounded, although the lone plane, a Junkers 88, had been clearly visible for several minutes before its bombs were dropped.

The stick fell on the hill's tightly packed terraced houses, homes

The scene of devastation on Albion Hill. St Bartholomew's Church, seen in the background, emerged from the war unscathed.

built for the working classes around the turn of the century. The worst of the damage was caused in Albion Hill, Cambridge Street and Ashton Street. Nearly thirty houses were wrecked or so badly damaged that they collapsed shortly afterwards, or had to be demolished. Minor damage was caused to houses over a wide area and streets in a quarter mile radius were littered with broken glass.

Rescue work went on until nearly midnight as tons of debris had to be cleared in the search for trapped victims.

Two heavy calibre bombs, possibly 500kg, were dropped, one crashing down at the junction of Albion Hill and Ashton Street. This landed on and demolished a butcher's shop, killing the owner William Chubb. Also killed was fifty seven year old Nellie Vincent of 13 Albion Hill. She had been pulled from her wrecked home alive, but died later that day at Brighton General Hospital.

The second bomb landed in a garden, wrecking houses in Cambridge Street and Dinapore Street.

An oil bomb also fell close by and exploded. It made a direct hit on a house at the junction of Cambridge Street and Albion Hill, bursting and showering the houses on the opposite side of the road in a huge cascade of crude oil. Several streets had to be evacuated and shut off, and workers in nearby Tamplins Brewery were also evacuated.

The vast majority of the injured were the children who had been playing in the streets. They were taken to both the Royal Sussex County Hospital and Brighton General Hospital. One boy, in his home in Ashton Street, was flung across a basement room on the chair in which he was sitting. He rushed from the house, is said to have rescued an elderly woman from a house opposite, then returned to his own home and rescued his sixty five year old grandmother from the debris.

In all thirty three houses were demolished as well as the Sir John Falstaff pub at 137 Albion Hill.

As rescue work progressed the Bishop of Lewes, Hugh Horden, and the Mayor and Mayoress of Brighton, J Talbot Nanson and Mrs D Scott- Prime, toured the area, talking to residents and comforting them. Temporary accommodation for some of the families made homeless was provided at the Salvation Army's Congress Hall, and the Connaught Institute in Lewes Road.

Mary Wille (now Mrs Bailey, of New Zealand) lived at 27 Cambridge Street with her parents, sister Connie and eighteen month old brother Walter. When the bombs fell Mary was at Varndean School. She remembers being taken home by the police to find the house just a ruin. Her arthritic grandfather, Henry Corrigan, who had been visiting the family, had escaped with Mary's mother and then torn desperately at the rubble to find and bring out the baby.

The family were sheltered at Congress Hall overnight and when they returned to their wrecked home the following day to salvage what they could, German fighters appeared overhead and machine gunned them. Terrified, they lay in the gutter and covered their heads with their hands, expecting death at any minute.

**KILLED AS A RESULT OF ENEMY ACTION
ON TUESDAY SEPTEMBER 24 1940**

CHUBB William, 52, 174 Hollingdean Terrace,
in his butcher's shop in Albion Hill.
VINCENT Nellie, 57, 13 Albion Hill, in BGH.

SATURDAY OCTOBER 26 1940

A SINGLE German aircraft flew so low over the town centre, at about 1pm, that a woman who saw it thought it must be an allied plane.

She lived close to the house in Egremont Place that was bombed by the raider and although she did not hear the explosion, the blast knocked her across the room into the wall opposite.

It could be that the aircraft had been damaged by fighters and, flying low, released its cargo in a bid to gain height and escape across the Channel.

The bomb fell on an unoccupied house in Egremont Place, totally destroying it and partially destroying No. 20 next door. No air raid warning had been sounded.

Arthur Betts, the elderly occupier of No. 20, was rescued alive from the debris of his home, but he died later that day from his injuries at the Royal Sussex County Hospital.

As the collapsed masonry was cleared, the body of Arthur's daughter Mary was found. Two hours later a faint voice was heard from the basement area. A woman called to rescuers that she was badly injured and was suffering a lot of pain. It was Mary Payne, Arthur's seventy five year old sister in law, who also lived at 20 Egremont Place. She had been in the back room of the ground floor and as the house collapsed she had fallen with it to the basement scullery. She was taken to hospital, released after a few weeks, but died on December 10.

The same German plane dropped an oil bomb on playing fields near Sutherland Road, causing no damage apart from a large crater, and another bomb landed in a nearby garden, causing minimal damage apart from broken windows and roof slates.

KILLED AS A RESULT OF ENEMY ACTION ON SATURDAY OCTOBER 26 1940

BETTS Arthur Thomas, 76, 20 Egremont Place.
BETTS Mary Cecilia, 45, 20 Egremont Place.
PAYNE Mary Louise, 75, 20 Egremont Place, on December 10.

A crowd gathers to see the damage on the morning after Hanningtons,
Brighton's most prestigious department store, was hit.

FRIDAY NOVEMBER 29 1940

IT WAS a typical November evening – chilly, with fog, swirling mist
and a light wind. At about 9.30pm an unknown number of enemy aircraft blanketted the town centre with incendiary bombs, followed by
possibly four high explosive bombs. Once again the warning sirens
were late in sounding.

East Street bore the brunt of the attack with one bomb causing serious damage to Lyon and Hall, the music shop on the west side of the
street. A number of expensive pianos were wrecked and the shop was
set on fire. Further along East Street Hanningtons suffered serious
damage. Other East Street shops were fired by the incendiaries but the
swift action of ARP personnel kept damage to a minimum.

One of the incendiary bombs crashed through the roof of the Savoy
Cinema and fell into a corner of the auditorium. The audience and

the staff of the cinema showed amazing coolness and although the whole of the interior was lit up, nobody was hurt,' said a newspaper report. 'All but a few patrons, close to where the bomb fell, retained their seats and the showing of the film was not interrupted.' The manager told the reporter that there was not the slightest panic of any kind.

Another bomb fell in Black Lion Lane, damaging the back of one house. One resident had a lucky escape. She had been lying in bed when the explosion tilted the bed, covering it with rubble and dust. Her rescuers had to saw through roof beams to release her.

Small fires were also caused in properties in Cannon Place, Western Road, Clifton Road and Victoria Road. The Clock Tower at the top of North Street was shattered and the hands and parts of the mechanism were picked up from the pavement.

Despite the ferocity of the raid, nobody was killed

WEDNESDAY DECEMBER 11 1940

THIS became known as Brighton's luckiest air raid. At 8.50pm a number of German fighter bombers (official reports estimate seven) attacked Newhaven and then Brighton. They had been part of a massive raid on Birmingham, but for some reason these seven changed their target.

It was a moonlit night with little cloud. The sirens were sounded and it was not long before the crump and explosions of falling bombs were heard. The 500kg bombs, among the largest dropped on Brighton during the war, fell on business and residential properties in Ship Street, Western Road and Upper North Street.

Four were dropped, but all four failed to explode – hence the 'lucky' raid.

Chief shelter warden Bill Mather called to offer help to a woman in Upper North Street after one of the bombs had fallen through her roof. 'Is there anything I can do here?' he called out through the choking black dust and debris. 'Yes,' came the angry reply. 'Come and see what the so and so has done to my geyser!'

Many people suffered minor injuries; two were taken to hospital while others were treated at local first aid posts.

Bomb disposal units arrived in town to defuse the bombs, meanwhile people living within a wide area of the town centre were evacuated until the bombs had been made safe.

Although lucky for Brighton this same raid was Newhaven's worst. Before arriving over Brighton one of the bombers had attacked the port town and twelve people were killed – a tragedy put into perspective by the fact that only eighteen Newhaven people died in bombing raids throughout the six years of war.

Five of the dead were from one family. A sixteen year old boy lost both his parents and two sisters; he was seriously injured and taken to hospital in Brighton where he died five days later. The single bomb fell on Folly Fields in Lewes Road.

4

THE FIRE SERVICES FIGHT BACK

SUNDAY MARCH 9 1941

IT WAS a clear, bright night, and the drone of aircraft had been clearly heard for some minutes an hour or so before midnight. Shortly afterwards the calm was shattered by screaching, ear piercing whistling as bombs started to fall on Preston Village.

It was a particularly ferocious attack, but one that showed ever increasing investment in firefighting training was paying off, and that the danger posed by incendiary bombs was now within manageable proportions. But before that night was out the firemen would need all their skills.

Witnesses estimated that eleven high explosive bombs fell, striking houses in Preston Road and Lauriston Road, and damaging properties in North Road, Home Road and Cumberland Road. These were followed by up to 300 incendiary bombs.

One of the bombs fell in Preston Road, just north of the junction with Preston Drove, almost opposite the bowling greens. The gas main was fractured, causing a large fire in the middle of the road. St John's Church suffered severe damage; part of a wall was demolished, another wall cracked and stained glass windows were shattered.

Another bomb struck the butcher's at 229 Preston Road where Fred and Madge Colbourne lived above the shop with their children Stella, Bill and Bernard. The bomb took out the front part of the building and the Colbournes, and their two young sons in the bedroom next door, plunged through two floors to be buried in the basement under

The pile of rubble to the left is the remains of the Colbourne family's butcher's shop and home in Preston Road and, below, some more shattered shops in the same area.

a mountain of masonry. Seventeen year old Stella, in a back bedroom, went to the door and saw just a hole where the house had been. She rushed to the window and shouted for help. Recalling the nightmare more than fifty years later, Stella said a soldier called for her to climb out and he would catch her. 'I was embarrassed about being in my nightdress. I tried to negotiate the space where the window had been, holding my nightie down with one hand. Then the soldier said "don't worry luv, I'm a married man". Of all that happened that night I can still remember, vividly, blushing when he said that.'

Two years later Stella married a Fleet Air Arm pilot and in 1947 went to live in Canada.

Rescuers could hear three year old Bernard crying under the debris. Then after a further subsidence the crying stopped.

'Where are you? In the basement?' called out rescuer Rinaldo 'Chris' Cristofoli (an Italian mosaic floor installer, who had lived in England since he was a child). 'No, upstairs you bloody fool,' replied the badly injured butcher, unaware that the building had collapsed upon him.

It took two hours to reach the family. Bernard was dead, Fred Colbourne had a fractured pelvis and Madge and Bill were lucky to escape with just cuts and bruises.

Bill, who was five when the bomb destroyed his home and killed his brother, recalled many years later that he had had 'a sort of yearning allied to a sense of foreboding' that day. Although he had been in St John's Church only once, for Bernard's christening, he asked to go to church that Sunday. His request was not taken seriously, but the little boy persisted and a reluctant Stella was persuaded to take him to the evening service. Halfway through he burst into tears and had to be taken home.

He and Bernard were asleep in the same bed when the bomb fell. 'My impression was that the coalman had come and emptied a sack of coal on top of me,' Bill said. 'It was very frightening. I wavered between consciousness and unconsciousness for what seemed an eternity.'

Rescued eventually, Bill was taken to an ambulance with the body of his little brother. 'I remember seeing an awful bruise on his temple. I did not know then that he was dead,' Bill said.

The Colbourne's wire haired terrier Biddy was seen scrabbling about in the ruins of the shop for several days afterwards, but then she disappeared and was never seen again.

Also hit and demolished were 227 Preston Road, an unoccupied dairy, 231 Preston Road, Frank Kirby's grocery shop, and another grocery, Gravely's, at 225 Preston Road.

John Stone and his wife Mary lived in the flat above Gravelys. His body was recovered from the wreckage of his home and his wife was pulled out alive and taken to hospital seriously injured.

Within a few minutes of this attack, and as the main group of rescue workers arrived, the incendiaries began raining down like confetti. Most fell in gardens and open spaces and were quickly dealt with. In some instances they landed on roofs but were extinguished before fire could take hold. One woman was seen in her nightdress extinguishing an incendiary bomb with a sandbag and shovel.

One of these incendiaries fell on 13 Gordon Road, home of elderly couple Harry and Emma Temple. They had just finished their supper of bread and cheese when Harry, realising a raid of some consequence was in progress, took a look around before going to bed and spotted a bright white line under the larder door. He opened it and found an incendiary bomb had crashed through the lean-to roof and the larder was well alight. When a bowl of water failed to extinguish it Harry picked up a large round cake tin and hurled it at the bomb, which then expired.

The following day was Harry's birthday and Emma had secretly saved their ration of fats and scarce commodities for weeks to make him a birthday cake – and it was in that cake tin. When the tin was opened it revealed a small cinder of pure carbon.

The death total for such a savage attack was just two, with thirteen injured.

KILLED AS A RESULT OF ENEMY ACTION
ON SUNDAY MARCH 9 1941
COLBOURNE Bernard, 3, 229 Preston Road.
STONE John Alan, 61, 225 Preston Road.

TUESDAY MARCH 11 1941

A LONE enemy aircraft dropped four 250kg bombs in the Freshfield Road area at about 10pm. One wrecked two houses in Dawson Terrace, burying the occupants of No. 5, and rescuers were hampered because the houses were on a steep hill.

It was an hour and a half before Ernest and Laura Burnet-Smith were released from the ruins of their home. They were rushed to the Royal Sussex County Hospital close by, but Mr Burnet-Smith was dead on arrival. His wife suffered shock and a number of minor injuries.

A second bomb struck a house in Freshfield Road, near the junction with Queens Park Terrace, causing considerable damage but miraculously with no serious injuries to the three occupants, who were treated at the local first aid post.

The third bomb also fell in Freshfield Road, causing a large crater, and the fourth fell on allotments north east of Dawson Terrace, at a place known then as Bakers Bottom.

Some incendiaries were also dropped, but fell mainly on open spaces where they were dealt with by local fire fighters and passers-by.

**KILLED AS A RESULT OF ENEMY ACTION
ON TUESDAY MARCH 11 1941**

BURNET-SMITH Ernest Joseph, 53,
5 Dawson Terrace.

A 73 year old pensioner died when her home in St George's Terrace
received a direct hit in the early hours of April 19, 1941.

5

THE RESCUE THAT WENT WRONG

WEDNESDAY APRIL 9 1941

HERBERT Morrison, the Minister of Home Security, was questioned in the wake of the raid that devastated Brighton in the small hours of this spring morning. There was an outcry from the townsfolk; newspapers were inundated with angry letters and a strongly worded petition was sent to Whitehall.

The reason for this violent eruption of feeling was the fate of the Wallis family, buried beneath the ruins of their Norfolk Square home for fifty six hours.

It was half an hour after midnight when aircraft were heard overhead, and the pips sounded simultaneously. Vapour trails were clearly visible in the bright moonlit sky.

The raiders came in from the sea, having crossed the Channel at very low level to dodge radar and coastal defences. Bombs began to fall but, for some unexplained reason, the explosions seemed less loud and many Brightonians slept through the raid, oblivious to what had happened.

It is believed that some twenty high explosive bombs were dropped on the town, but the most serious damage, injury and loss of life occurred in Norfolk Square. There was death and destruction, too, in George Street Gardens, Edward Street, Grosvenor Street, St George's Terrace and Hereford Street.

Stories abound of people escaping practically unscathed from the ruins of their homes that night. A woman of eighty was safely rescued from the upper floor of her badly damaged home; from the wreckage of a neighbouring house a blind woman got out unharmed, and a man in his nineties was rescued by the matron of a home. A young woman and a man on the top floor of a boarding house in Norfolk Square fell to the street on top of the collapsing wreckage and were picked up suffering nothing more serious than shock and scratches.

The Wallis family, who had arrived in Brighton as evacuees, lived at 8 Norfolk Square. When the bomb that destroyed their home fell Mr Wallis was in hospital recovering from an operation. In the house were Violet, forty three, and their four children – Robert, twelve, Rose, eleven, Jean, six and Audrey, three.

Fifty six hours after their home collapsed around them, a policeman heard a faint call coming from the ruins; it was Violet. 'Save my baby,' she cried. Help was summoned and rescuers dug valiantly, reaching the trapped woman, and Jean, still alive, after two hours. Clasped in Violet's arms was three year old Audrey who had been killed instantly, but the tiny body retained some warmth through being pressed so long against her mother. Rescuers then found the bodies of the two other children.

For almost two and a half days Violet, injured, desperate to know the fate of her children, believing that Audrey still lived, had lain beneath the remains of a four storey house – while the rescue team suspended work at 7pm on two successive days, with an hour and a half of daylight still remaining, and did not return to the site until 7am the following day, an hour and a half after daylight.

Brightonians were outraged. An inquiry was set up and the official outcome was that because the building was in such a dangerous state, with its one remaining wall liable to collapse at any moment, it had been deemed inadvisable to risk the men's lives, and it was not thought that any of the buried victims remained alive. The matter was raised in Parliament by Sir Cooper Rawson MP, and Mr Morrison agreed that because 'public anxiety had been so widespread' a careful inquiry into the situation would be made.

There were rows in Brighton council chamber about the scandal, with accusations flying as to who was responsible for giving the order to cease work. One councillor, accusing officers of keeping the council

Violet Wallis and her four children were trapped for two and a half days under the remains of houses in Norfolk Square because rescue workers clocked off early.

in the dark, demanded an explanation. Reporters were removed from the chamber when the council went into camera to discuss the situation – but there was never a satisfactory outcome. A statement was issued to the press later saying that the council had passed a resolution by a majority of forty four to four: 'That, having considered the incident. . . the members of the Council desire to express their most sincere sympathy with those who suffered on that occasion and desire further to express their fullest confidence in the Controller (of the ARP), the Borough Engineer, and the members of the Emergency Committee and Air Raid Precautions Committee. The Council are satisfied that the account of the matter given in the letter from the Master Builders' Association fairly and correctly represents what took place.'

The scandal stirred strong feelings in the town and there were angry letters in the local newspapers. One serviceman wrote saying 'Well, Brighton, it is up to you to wipe the slur from your name'. In

41

the remaining years of the war the Brighton rescue services did indeed wipe out the slur.

The same raid caused devastation across town, eastwards, where, meanwhile, frantic efforts were being made to rescue people buried in the debris of their homes. George Street Gardens near St James's Street suffered a direct hit, the bomb demolishing No. 14. The diggers eventually released Susan Harris, but her injuries were so severe that she died later that day in hospital. Recovered also were the bodies of Susan's daughter, Ivy, and that of Albert Gander whose home was 8 Windsor Street. Next door, in No. 13, was the body of Annie Peacock.

Not far away the pub at 101 Edward Street also received a direct hit, and adjacent properties suffered substantial damage. Pulled later from the wreckage were the bodies of the licensee Charles Pain, his wife Margaret and their seven year old grandson Ian Patterson.

Also killed were Cecil Shorter, an ambulance driver, who lived next door to the pub, and Elizabeth Parsons, at her home in Grosvenor Street.

In nearby Hereford Street. A bomb struck No. 13 and killed a family of four – Frederick and Elizabeth Young and their children, Alfred and Doris.

Down the road at 11 St George's Terrace Susan and Minnie Stops were killed, and at the same address an elderly woman, Lucy Eade, was rescued and taken to hospital where she died later the same day.

Back in Norfolk Square rescuers were still working

Rescuers working through the debris of the Norfolk Square houses.

through the mountains of debris from the large old Victorian houses that had collapsed. At No. 9 the bodies of Nathan Cassler and his three children were found. Neighbours cried as the remains of Edyce, sixteen, Brenda, eleven, and Natalie, five, were brought out.

The body of another resident of No 9, Rupert Calcraft, was also recovered.

KILLED ON AS A RESULT OF ENEMY ACTION WEDNESDAY APRIL 9 1941

CALCRAFT, Rupert Harold, 51,
9 Norfolk Square.
CASSLER Brenda, 11,
9 Norfolk Square.
CASSLER Edyce, 16,
9 Norfolk Square.
CASSLER Natalie Monica, 5,
9 Norfolk Square.
CASSLER Nathan, 47,
9 Norfolk Square.
EADE LUCY, 73, 11
St George's Terrace.
GANDER Albert, 62,
8 Windsor Street.
HARRIS Ivy Elizabeth, 18,
14 George Street Gardens.
HARRIS Susan, 52,
14 George Street Gardens.
PAINE Charles, 63,
101 Edward Street.
PAINE Margaret Louise, 63,
101 Edward Street.
PARSONS Elizabeth, 54,
49 Grosvenor Street.

PATTERSON Ian Robert, 7,
101 Edward Street.
PEACOCK Annie Elizabeth, 61,
52 Richmond Street.
SHORTER Cecil Reginald, 51,
100 Edward Street.
STOPS Minnie, 45,
11 St George's Terrace.
STOPS Susan Wakefield, 64,
11 St George's Terrace.
WALLIS Audrey, 3,
8 Norfolk Square.
WALLIS Robert, 12,
8 Norfolk Square.
WALLIS Rose, 11,
8 Norfolk Square.
YOUNG Alfred Arthur, 17,
13 Hereford Street.
YOUNG Doris May, 15,
13 Hereford Street.
YOUNG Elizabeth, 49,
13 Hereford Street.
YOUNG Frederick, 49,
13 Hereford Street.

MONDAY MAY 18 1941

THREE ME 109s swept in from the sea at 8pm. They were flying low and released their 250kg bombs from a height of only 250 feet.

Immediately after their south east to north west bombing run the aircraft turned south and disappeared quickly across the Channel – but not before havoc was caused by cannon shells and machine gun fire from the raiders.

There had been no time to sound the general alarm, but a local alert had been given at 8.06pm. Nobody was killed, but nine people suffered slight injuries, and fifty five houses were damaged.

The first bomb fell in the north east corner of the corporation yard in Hollingdean Road, bounced off a pile of steel girders and exploded on the second impact close to the dust destructor. Fragments of metal machinery were thrown for distances up to 300 feet.

The second bomb fell on earth banking alongside the south parapet wall of the railway viaduct over London Road. A forty two feet length of parapet was demolished, also forty feet of retaining wall below the tracks.

The third bomb did the most damage, falling on the signal and telegraph section of the railway engineers' department close to the eastern platform at Brighton Station. The whole of the west wall, with a seventy two feet frontage, was blown out and the factory was completely destroyed. The debris blocked two railway lines. The roof caught fire, as did the signal box.

There was only one casualty, a woman, who was taken to hospital suffereing from severe shock.

TUESDAY JUNE 1 1942

AN unidentified German aircraft was seen, in clear moonlight, to cross the coastline at Bognor Regis at 3.35am. It was flying at a height of approximately 6,000 feet in a north easterly direction towards Lewes. Suddenly it turned southwards, flying as far as Rottingdean before it turned again, this time westwards, and the pilot began his bombing run.

Four 250kg bombs were dropped in a group and the aircraft sped off in a south westerly direction. The attack had lasted little more than a minute. Three of the bombs fell in a corn field, close to each other, north west of Moulescoomb Place, making three large craters. The fourth fell harmlessly on Downland ninety feet away.

The target, it was thought, was the railway viaduct over Lewes Road some 300 yards away.

SATURDAY JUNE 26 1942

FLYING very low, at barely 150 feet, two ME 109s approached Brighton from the south at 9.48pm. As they crossed the coast at Black Rock they fired their cannons at the Marine Gate flats and the nearby gasometers.

As quickly as they had come the aircraft left, turning south and west out to sea. The incident had lasted just fifteen seconds, but the damage caused was described as 'telling'. Anti aircraft guns on Marine Parade had opened fire and possibly frightened them off.

At the gas company's Black Rock depot a gasometer holding 711,000 cubic feet of gas was hit. Escaping gas ignited and was lost, and the gasometer was destroyed. Firemen, using ten hose reels, toiled until close to midnight before the inferno was under control.

The seven storey block of flats was struck by twenty two shells that failed to pierce the building, but which caused extensive damage to the front wall. Fragments of one shell caused some damage in one room and a number of windows were shattered. Also damaged were four houses in Riflebutt Road, and workshops and storehouses in the gas company compound.

THURSDAY JULY 22 1942

SEAFRONT defences opened up when two ME 109s, flying abreast, were spotted approaching the coastline opposite the Royal Crescent Hotel. They were very low, about 150–200 feet above the sea. The time was 11.14am. Although it was close to midsummer, the weather was dull, with a strong south westerly wind.

Just before reaching land the aircraft turned westward and each dropped a 250kg bomb. One fell into the sea fifty yards to the west of the Palace Pier; the other dropped right up against the east of the pier, close to the theatre at the end. For security reasons both piers had been severed in the middle – to prevent a seaward invasion – and at the time it was difficult to check the full extent of the damage. From the land end it was estimated that the pier suffered blast damage to the timber superstructure and glass panels of the theatre.

Yet more damage to the Marine Gate flats – the most heavily attacked building in Brighton

SATURDAY AUGUST 29 1942

TWO enemy fighter bombers made a low dive over Brighton, attacking firstly with machine gun and cannon fire, then dropping one bomb each. It was shortly after lunch, at 2.19pm, when they were first spotted. As the raiders turned to flee seafront defences opened up and British fighters appeared in hot pursuit. One of the enemy planes was said to be smoking from the tail as it lost height and disappeared.

The first bomb to fall landed close to Marine Gate flats on Marine Drive. Hundreds of windows were blown out by the force of the explosion, doors were ripped from their hinges and furniture was badly damaged. Many of the residents were made homeless.

The only person killed was twenty year old Claudette Mawby who lived with her mother and sisters in Flat B7. Her body was found at the bottom of the lift shaft. It was thought likely that Claudette had been blown through the metal casing of the lift door on one of the floors.

Claudette and her twin sister 'Coy', and an older sister Angela, had been well known child stars in Hollywood. The family had moved into the flat just three days before the bombing. Mrs Mawby and Angela were among those injured. The porter, twenty year old John Shanahan, was also injured. Apart from the havoc caused by the bomb blast, the building was also severely damaged by machine gun bullets.

7

SNEAK RAID CARNAGE

MONDAY OCTOBER 12 1942
SHORTLY before 12.30pm on this autumn day, four Focke-Wulf 190s approached Brighton from the south, crossing the coast at about 150 feet. The day was cloudy and overcast, giving the enemy good cover. Air raid sirens were sounded at 12.27pm, minutes after the planes had been spotted.

Each dropped a 500kg bomb on the town centre, killing and injuring a number of people at a time when the streets were crowded with shoppers and workers going to lunch. Taken by surprise, they had no time to find shelter.

Members of the Royal Observer Corps at the Rottingdean post said afterwards that the first they knew that a raid was in progress was when the heard the first bomb exploding, timed at 12.24pm. Within a few seconds they saw the enemy aircraft coming west, apparently straight for their post, but then the pilots spotted people walking in the grounds of St Dunstans, the home for blind ex- servicemen, at Ovingdean, and they opened up with cannon and machine gun fire, killing one man, John Dudeney. At the time the planes were not much more than 100 feet above the clifftop. Immediately the Focke-Wulfs turned seaward and fled.

Buckingham Close, a block of flats at the junction of Buckingham Place and Bath Street, was hit by the first bomb. The rear of the block was completely demolished and three people were killed - Joseph and Florence Shepherd, an elderly couple, and Lydia Townend. The blast damaged houses in the next road, Compton Avenue, and William Ford and Maria Williamson died in number 21.

The second bomb landed in the roadway of Howard Place, 250 feet

AFTER THE BOMBING OF OCTOBER 12 1942

The first bomb hit the flats in Buckingham Close and, below, inside St Anne's Home for disabled and invalid children after the raid.

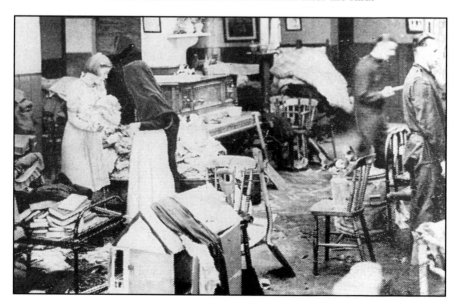

The devastation caused to Elder Place by the third bomb and, below, the fourth bomb did this to Rose Hill Terrace.

from the junction with Buckingham Place. It skidded, cutting a wide groove in the road, and detonated on the wall at the top of the cliffs above the railway, just north of Brighton Station. A thirty feet length of wall was thrown on to the track damaging five locomotives, six coaches and six wagons.

Tragically, the same bomb caused death and injury at St Anne's Home for disabled and invalid children in Buckingham Place. Twenty one children were playing in the garden when the bomb struck, and two year old Anthony Leadbetter was killed instantly. Many of the children in the garden were injured, as were children inside the building where considerable damage was caused. Another nineteen children in the neighbourhood were also hurt, the youngest being an eleven week old boy whose mother succeeded in snatching him from his cot as the roof of her house fell in.

The third bomb fell in Elder Place, striking a rear garden wall and demolishing a surface shelter and four houses. Seventy year old Florence Shorrocks of 16 Elder Place was rescued, but was badly injured and died in Brighton General Hospital on October 23. The fourth bomb hit 64–67 Rose Hill Terrace, just east of the junction with Kingsbury Road, destroying all of the houses and severely damaging two others opposite. Edith Orme at 63 Rose Hill Terrace died and eleven people, including four children, were injured.

Nine died and thirty three were seriously injured on this day, and another sixty seven people sustained slight injuries. More than 250 houses were damaged.

KILLED AS A RESULT OF ENEMY ACTION ON MONDAY OCTOBER 12 1942

DUDENEY John, 55, 6 New Cottages, Ovingdean.
FORD William, 37, 31c Compton Avenue.
LEADBETTER Anthony Vincent, 2, St Anne's Home, Buckingham Place.
ORME Edith, 75, 63 Rose Hill Terrace.
SHEPHERD Florence, 72, 24 Buckingham Close.
SHEPHERD Francis Joseph, 70, 24 Buckingham Close.
SHORROCKS Florence Augusta, 70, 16 Elder Place.
TOWNEND Lydia Boardman, 76, 26 Buckingham Close,
WILLIAMSON Maria, 73, 31c Compton Avenue.

FRIDAY DECEMBER 18 1942

ROTTINGDEAN suffered its first attack on a wet December morning shortly before noon.

A Dornier 217 came in from the south at around 200 feet above sea level. It turned east and flew along the coastline then banked north eastwards towards Rottingdean. Over the village it dropped its payload of four 500kg bombs.

One hit the six storey steel framed St Margarets building, which had shops on the ground floor and flats above. The bomb exploded on the fifth floor causing floors and partition walls to collapse. The shops below, and a cafe, were badly damaged by falling debris.

At the time most of the residents were out, but there were a few minor injuries among those who were at home. Two women were taken to hospital and others received treatment at the first aid post.

War reserve policeman Harold Stone, who had recently moved from London, was on duty at the crosroads and was struck by fragments of debris. He was rushed to hospital where he died later that day.

The second bomb hit the playing field and ricocheted from there to explode in front of St Margaret's Vicarage in Steyning Road. The front wall of the house collapsed and the only occupant, the maid, was quickly rescued from the ruins, suffering severe shock, minor cuts and scratches.

The third bomb also fell in the playing field and then bounced over a nearby house and into a garden. Fortunately it did not explode and was dealt with by a bomb disposal squad.

Headstone on the grave of Harold Stone, killed at Rottingdean on December 18.

The final bomb again fell in the field, ricocheted and exploded in the grounds of the Tudor House Hotel. A gardener was cut on the head and face by flying glass from a shattered greenhouse.

After dropping its bombs the Dornier turned and flew over Ovingdean and Kemp Town, where it opened fire with its machine guns but caused little damage.

Shortly after the attack a New Zealand fighter pilot reported that he had sighted a Dorner 217 flying at 400–500 feet above the sea, a few miles south of Brighton, and had given chase. He saw his bullets hit the fuselage and the starboard wing, and after that smoke started to pour from the underside of the wing. The plane dived down to sea level but pulled upwards into the clouds again. The New Zealander followed and caught three further glimpses of the enemy before he lost it and returned to base.

Later that day the wreckage of a Dornier 217 was found in the sea but there were no survivors.

SATURDAY FEBRUARY 13 1943

AT a minute before 9pm on a cold, dark winter night, a single enemy aircraft, thought to have been a Dornier 217, dropped ten bombs on Woodingdean, some of them being incendiaries.

They all landed within a radius of about seventy five yards halfway between the southern side of Crescent Drive South and an area of open ground known as the Bostle. Blast damage was caused to several houses, but residents received only minor injuries.

Some thought, at the time, that the crew had deliberately dropped the bombs on open land so that there would be little or no damage to property and no loss of life.

The municipal fruit and vegetable market in Circus Street, struck by a bomb that
went right through it and exploded in the school clinic. *Photo: PRO, Kew.*

8

THE CLINIC IS BOMBED

MONDAY MARCH 29 1943

LIKE the attack that became known as 'the day they bombed the
Odeon', the raid on this March morning was always known afterwards
as 'the day they bombed the clinic'.

It was 11.08am when four Focke-Wulf 190s made a sudden low level
swoop from the sea as the sirens sounded. The town centre streets
were raked with cannon and machine gun fire before bombs began to
rain down. One struck the municipal fruit and vegetable market in
Circus street, travelled northwards through the building, killing
Stanley Bowles, penetrated the north wall, crossed the street and

53

exploded in the school clinic in Sussex Street (now Morley Street). Miraculously the Monday morning session at the clinic was very quiet. There were a few expectant mothers attending for the ante natal clinic and a handful of children there for dental treatment.

Two of the three children killed were Rose Mary Fenson, ten, and her eight year old brother Ronald, who had been playing on the steps of the clinic while their pregnant mother was inside. The family lived at 44 Cheltenham Place, almost the exact spot where the second bomb fell. The third child victim was Jose Sayers, aged six.

The doctor who had been attending Mrs Fenson emerged from the debris with just minor injuries, but covered in dust and grime, and he started work immediately treating those who had been injured. And the senior dentist, although suffering from a badly cut hand, helped with the rescue work and it was late in the afternoon before he allowed his wounds to be treated.

Robert Ticehurst, the chief clerk, was buried in the wreckage of his office and was found to be dead when rescuers reached him during the latter part of the afternoon. His assistant, Jean Carter, twenty one, was dug out alive and although in considerable pain from back injuries, she smiled and waved to onlookers as she was taken to the ambulance.

The rescue services paid a particular tribute to Peter Brassington, a twenty year old Jamaican telegraphist in the Royal Navy, who worked tirelessly for more than two hours helping to rescue and comfort the injured. He had been in the country for only six months and this was his first experience of an air attack.

Another bomb demolished the northern half of the Baptist church in Gloucester Place, and it was counted a miracle that although there were a number of people inside, nobody was killed. Properties near the church, including a motor showroom, a cafe and small flats, were reduced to rubble. And a large building divided into flats was so badly damaged that it had to be demolished.

The rescue work here posed a more difficult problem than at the clinic. Because the building had been so tall the pile of debris was much higher. Sound location meters were used to trace victims trapped underneath and at about 5pm, some six hours after the raid,

Rescue workers searching for survivors in the wreckage of the clinic.
Photo: Brighton Reference Library.

the rescuers had their first success when two small girls were brought out, dirty and dishevelled but with only slight injuries.

Locally based Canadian soldiers joined the rescue services in Gloucester Place, spending many hours digging in the rubble. A bomb also fell on Grosvenor Street, off Edward Street – an area that suffered time after time in the raids on Brighton. No. 8 was wrecked but twelve year old Jimmy Southon owed his life to the fact that he had been lying in the Morrison shelter, having been kept home from school as he felt unwell.

Masonry engulfed his shelter but he managed to escape and his frightened calls were heard by Civil Defence rescuers who quickly pulled him out. His mother Harriet, and another woman, Caroline Cotton, were later found dead in the rubble.

The enemy aircraft made off westwards towards Hove, flying low and machine gunning people in the streets. Two more bombs were dropped, one hitting a printing works and the other crashing through a house into the basement.

Spitfires from 610 Squadron based at Biggin Hill pursued the raiders – which were from 10 Staffel Jagdgeschwader 53. One, number 2576, piloted by twenty one year old Obergefreiter Joachim Koch, was shot down over the sea at 11.15am 500 yards off Brighton beach. Koch's body as washed ashore at Ovingdean on Sunday, April 25. He was buried in Bear Road cemetery.

KILLED AS A RESULT OF ENEMY ACTION ON MONDAY MARCH 29 1943

BETTESWORTH Florence Emily, 46, 20 Gloucester Place.

BOWLES Stanley Albert, 39, 30 Woodland Avenue.

COTTON Caroline, 68, 35 Upper Park Place.

EADE James Arthur, 4 months, 21 Gloucester Place, at BGH on April 19.

EADE Muriel Gwendoline, 27, 21 Gloucster Place.

FENSON Ronald, 8, 44 Cheltenham Place.

FENSON Rose Mary, 10, 44 Cheltenham Place.

HARDWICK Rosetta Alice, 33, 11 Grosvenor Street.

McALLISTER David, 54, 31 Sussex Street

MILLER- MACKAY Hugh, 68, 21 Gloucester Place, at RSCH on April 22

NEWGERITZ Verena Mary Elizabeth, 54, 26 Park Road, Coldean.

NEWMAN Ruby Emily, 13 months, 11 Grosvenor Street.

PARR Elizabeth, 81, 21 Gloucester Place.

RICHARDSON Mary Elizabeth, 63, 13 Grosvenor Street.

SAYERS Jose Clara, 6, 3 Hollingdean Road.

SOUTHON Harriet Elizabeth, 52, 8 Grosvenor Street.

TICEHURST Robert Ernest, 37, 64 Mayfield Crescent.

WHITE Philip Rampton, 26, 297 Hangleton Road, Hove, at his parents' home 20 Gloucester Place.

KOCH Joachim, 21, German pilot, shot down over the sea.

9

A TIME OF TERROR

TUESDAY MAY 25 1943

THE day of Brighton's worst air attack was warm and sunny and at just after midday workers were enjoying their lunch breaks in the parks and gardens and mothers were preparing food for their children - there were no school meals at this time.

At 12.20pm the warning was given, the pips system indicating that raiders were imminent. Almost immediately ten Focke-Wulf 190s crossed the coast at Rottingdean in line abreast, and another fifteen came in from the Channel in waves of three abreast one and a half miles east of the Palace Pier. All were no more than fifty feet above the sea and they rose to 150–200 feet to circle the town. The Bofors guns all along the seafront went into action and one plane was shot down as it approached the coast, crashing into the sea.

There was confusion on the ground because some of the enemy planes were painted grey, some were light green and yet others were silver grey. All the cowlings were painted black and one plane had two yellow stripes on the underside of its wings. The Swastika signs on all were said to be very faint.

In the space of just a few minutes terror and suffering were brought to hundreds of families; twenty four people were killed, fifty eight seriously injured and another sixty nine suffered slighter injuries. Seventeen homes were damaged by cannon and machine gun fire and 150 were made uninhabitable.

Almost 600 people were made homeless.

It was a typical hit and run raid, but pressed home with more than the usual vigour. Brighton people remember that the sky seemed full of German bombers, flying in all directions, amid deafening noise both from the screaming engines, the Bofors guns on the seafront and the naval guns in Sussex Square. The ambulance service was at full stretch, ferrying people to the town's two hospitals where many of the injured were left lying on stretchers in corridors, and all available off duty doctors and nurses were called in to help cope with the casualties.

The air over Brighton was heavy with thick, choking dust; each time the debris of wrecked buildings was moved great clouds billowed up and there was a particular smell that rescuers had come to recognise - the stench of death.

Extensive damage was caused in the Whitehawk Road area, the vicinity that had suffered in the very first attack on Brighton in July 1940. At the Whitehawk Road/Arundel Road crossroads PC Frank Barker, the local beat policeman, had just seen children across the road from St Mark's School.

He stood talking to Mr Rose, the local grocer, whose shop was at the corner of Whitehawk Road and Bristol Gardens. They both heard a bomb falling and quickly dropped to the ground, with PC Kenneth Grinstead, a motorcycle officer who was delivering daily orders to PC Barker. When the dirt and dust cleared Mr Rose shakily regained his feet – but the two policemen was dead. PC Barker had taken the full blast of the bomb that fell on the school playground and was dead.

PC Grinstead had been posting orders on a notice board on the wall of Wilson's Laundry. He was seriously injured in the bomb blast and taken to the Royal Sussex County Hospital where he died later the same day. Four days later his wife gave birth to a son, John.

Twenty minutes earlier the children had left for their midday break, but a few teachers were still in the school and one, Marion De Witt, was badly hurt. She was rushed to hospital where she died later that day.

Two workmen at a bench near Marine Gate had a miraculous escape when a 500kg bomb fell just outside the small building in which they were working. The bomb bounced, cutting through a wall, where it left its fin tail, and passed over the heads of the men, exiting through the roof at the other side of the building. It then exploded in the property next door. Neither of the men suffered any injuries.

The gas works at Black Rock was again a target and a bomb landed

PC Kenneth Grinstead
Photo: John Grinstead.

PC Frank Barker.
Photo: Mrs Dulcie Wisdom.

One of the wrecked gasholders at Black Rock

twenty two feet north of the valve house, just missing a gas holder. It ricocheted through the valve house wall and travelled about ninety seven feet before going through the roof on the south west. It then passed over the store house, where it was seen by the storeman, and vanished. The bomb failed to explode and was never found. It was believed at the time that it went out to sea.

Bombs were dropped over a wide area, including Preston Road, the railway station, Downs Terrace, Bath Street, Park Crescent, Bennett Road and Marine Gate – again. In all, twenty one bombs fell, all believed to be of 500kg. The last one was released at around 150 feet and its initial impact was on the ridge of an asbestos and boarded roof of a single storey building in Campbell Road. It then deflected to an angle of thirty degrees and passed through a garden wall on the south side of Argyle Road, three feet above ground.

There was then a double impact on the road and the bomb was deflected upwards, passing through 2 Argyle Villas, entering over a semi-basement window, and leaving the house through a back window.

Incredibly the bomb travelled a further sixty feet, passed through the first floor of a two storey brick workshop, a former Baptist hall, a distance of twenty seven feet.

Still on the move it travelled another fifty two feet and struck the pier of the railway viaduct, fifteen feet above ground level. But it was still travelling, and deflected some ninety degrees horizontally and downwards to detonate at the foot of the next pier.

The railway track from Brighton to Lewes was left hanging in the air after the viaduct was bombed. *Photo: Newhaven Historical Society.*

Two of the arches of the viaduct collapsed and debris at the foot of it was piled thirty feet high.

In 2 Argyle Villas was a family of six, five of them children, and when the bomb whistled through their house they were sheltering under the concrete steps to the semi basement. The bomb had bounced in the road, gone through the house between the ground and first floors, travelling upwards, passed through two rooms and smashed out of the back wall on its way to destroying the viaduct. The house was completely wrecked but the only casualty was a canary.

The family's cat was found three days later wandering around the bomb site.

The house in Princes Terrace to which Annie Avis in her Morrison shelter was carried by the bomb blast.
Photo: PRO, Kew.

Reginald Allam, then a child of thirteen, remembers emerging with his family from their shelter to find the pie his mother had made for lunch still cooking in the gas stove.

When pensioner Annie Avis heard the air raid warning she took refuge in her Morrison shelter, which was in a rear ground floor room of her home at 17 Bennett Road. The house took a direct hit and as it collapsed the shelter was blown against the rear wall of the house in the next road, Princes Terrace. The shelter broke up and the top, folded in half, sliced into the house through a window space.

It was in a Morrison shelter like this that Annie Avis took shelter in her house in Bennett Road.

The Park Crescent Inn through which a bomb passed before exploding in two large houses across the road, killing two of the occupants. *Photo: PRO, Kew.*

The remaining portion of the shelter, and Mrs Avis's body, dropped into the garden at the base of the house. Four houses in Bennett Road were partly demolished, and many others were badly damaged.

One of the bombs went right through the Park Crescent Inn, travelled across the width of Park Crescent and exploded in two large houses, Nos. 24 and 25, where both Kathleen Denbigh and Violet Crelley were killed.

Because of the ferocity of the attack and the widespread chaos across the town the rescue services were at full stretch, helped by British and Canadian soldiers.

One of the most difficult rescues of the day was at Chichester Place where a bomb had demolished Nos. 17 and 19. Seventy eight year old Robert Cochrane, of No. 17, was buried under mountains of rubble. He was pulled out after twenty three hours and died in hospital later in the day. Alexander Brawn, seventy three, who lived two doors away, was also buried in debris and was dead when rescuers reached him.

Meanwhile another tragedy was taking place in the parade of small shops at the eastern end of Down Terrace. Seven people, including two children, died when three of the four shops received a direct hit. Only the butcher's shop remained, although badly damaged.

The butcher's wife, Winifred Pinkstone, was taken out quickly and pleaded with her rescuers to find her husband. Later, James Pinkstone was found, but he was dead.

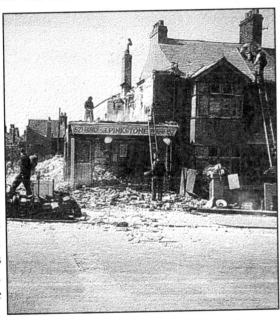

James Pinkstone's butcher's shop in Down Terrace.
Photo: PRO, Kew.

When the bomb fell Mrs Florence Goble was serving two boys in the grocery she ran with her husband, John. They were David Bell, eight, and William Eatwell, ten. All four were killed. At first it had been thought the children had survived, but as their bodies were pulled from the rubble women wept in the street.

Two young clergymen were among the first on the scene at Down Terrace. They helped to drag a man and a woman from one of the wrecked shops and then set about extricating another woman who, although badly injured, had survived.

In the parade there had also been a sweet shop run by Violet Eley. At the time there were two customers in the shop, a man and a fourteen year old boy, Reginald Fitch. Reginald had been asked by his sister to collect shoes from the cobbler. He had been given sixpence to spend and decided to call in at the sweet shop first. There was no loud bang, he remembered, but the whole building just caved in burying him, the customer and Mrs Eley.

He recalled: 'The first attempts at rescue were made by well meaning amateurs who climbed on to the wreckage, causing downward pressure on us. A neighbour, I believe his name was Jupp, a railway platelayer, saw the potential danger and organised the rescue by making a tunnel beneath the wreckage towards us. It was his voice that I first heard.

'Subsequently I learned that a girder had fallen on to a Lyons ice cream cabinet and we had been trapped in the space beneath. Undoubtedly without the cabinet being there we would have been crushed. I have since had a high regard for Lyons ice cream.

'I was told later that the mayor visited the scene and made a speech which was not well received. It was to the effect that "Brighton could take it". There was a public outcry about the lack of anti-aircraft defences and subsequently Marine Parade was lined with Bofors guns manned by Canadian soldiers who were a little trigger happy.'

The railway station and the tracks had been bombed before but on this day considerable damage was inflicted. There were three bombs, one on the track just north of Highcroft Villas, one near Dyke Road Drive and the third on the Pullman coach sheds. Two Pullman coaches were completely demolished and another twelve were damaged. Fifty ordinary coaches were damaged in the strike, four of them being telescoped into a tangled mass of twisted metal and glass.

One of the bombs that exploded on the railway track damaged goods wagons and the roofs of Nos 17 and 19 Dyke Road. *Photo: PRO, Kew.*

John Pearce was fatally injured in the railway station and died some hours later at Brighton General Hospital.

In Compton Road a bomb demolished four houses, in some of which soldiers were billeted. Frantically the rescuers dug through what remained of Nos. 20, 22, 24 and 26, finding some of the occupants quite quickly, but it was many hours before all were brought out. Miraculously only one person died – Mary Lloyd, of No. 24. Two houses on the opposite side of the road were badly damaged by the blast.

Yet again Marine Gate was hit. A 500kg bomb passed right through the fourth storey of the block, wrecking three flats; its fins were found wedged in the wooden floor of one of the flats. Many were injured but there were no fatalities. After passing through the building the bomb then apparently went out to sea as no further trace of it was found.

Another bomb aimed at the flats fell on waste ground close to the junction of Rottingdean Road and The Avenue.

It bounced at a right angle, ricocheted and hit a garage. It then passed right through the roof of a bungalow before bouncing again and slicing through Marine Gate, striking the southern side of Marine Drive where it exploded, causing damage to the water main.

Incredibly, the block of flats, still standing, was hit a third time when a bomb exploded against its south east corner, causing severe damage to the ground and first floors – where, at the time, repair work was being carried out after an earlier raid. Every remaining window in the block was shattered.

And again the gas works at Black Rock was targeted. A bomb went

The point of explosion of a bomb in one of the Marine Gate flats. *Photo: PRO, Kew.*

through two gas holders, setting them on fire. A third gas holder was split and escaping gas ignited, added to the existing roaring inferno, which kept the fire brigade at full stretch for many hours. As a result of this attack, some 2,750,000 cubic feet of gas was lost.

One of the bombs that day hit large Victorian residences in Eaton Place – Nos. 52, 54 and 56 and two elderly women were killed. They were Eliza Shepherd who was visiting friends at No. 52, and Lydia Shoosmith,

The Marine Gate flats somehow survived repeated attacks. The third bomb to hit them in this raid shattered every remaining window.
Photo: PRO, Kew.

who lived there.

The raid took five minutes. It left twenty four dead and 130 wounded. The enemy paid a price for the savage raid. Four of the twenty five FW 190s were destroyed – three sent crashing by anti aircraft fire and the fourth by an RAF Typhoon fighter.

Two days after the raid a newspaper reported: 'Fiften years ago businessman Mr Arthur Pratt lost a cheque and two postal orders. On

Tuesday he found them again. His premises were among those damaged in the raid. . . Going to his shop after the incident was over, he found them lying among the debris'. The explosions had dislodged the cheque and postal orders from whatever obscure hiding place they had fallen into in 1928.

KILLED AS A RESULT OF ENEMY ACTION ON TUESDAY MAY 25 1943

AVIS Annie, 61, 17 Bennett Road.
BARKER Frank William, 33,
7 Manor Road.
BELL David Keith, 8, 48 Freshfield
Road.
BRAWN Alexander, 73,
21 Chichester Place.
COCHRANE Allan, 78,
17 Chichester Place, at RSCH the
following day.
CRELLEY Violet, 39, 25 Park
Crescent.
DENBIGH Kathleen Louisa, 38,
24 Park Crescent, at 26a Park
Crescent.
DE- WITT Marion Eleanor, 66,
123 Preston Road.
EATWELL William Henry, 10,
4 Hallett Road.
ELEY Violet May, 43, 17 East Drive.
GOBLE Florence Elizabeth, 47,
58 Down Terrace.
GOBLE John James, 48,
58 Down Terrace.
GRINSTEAD Kenneth, 31,
234 Freshfield Road.
LLOYD Mary Anne, 52,
24 Compton Avenue.
OCKENDEN Leslie Albert, 33,
18 Coldean Lane.
PEARCE John Phillip, 48,
14 Cheltenham Place.
PINKSTONE James Robert, 48,
52 Down Terrace.
SEBBAGE Louisia Charlotte, 58,
23 Glynde Road, in Down Terrace.
SHAKESPEARE Percy, 36,
12 Maple Road, Priory, Dudley,
Worcestershire, at Marine Gate.
SHEPHERD Elizabeth, 68. 16
Rochester Street at 52 Eaton Place
SHOOSMITH Lydia, 78,
52 Eaton Place.
SIMMONDS Emma, 64,
15 Chesham Road.
THOMPSON George Edward, 43,
9 Nuthurst Road.
WALDER Nellie Amelia, 41,
66 Twineham Road, in Chesham
Road.

The interior wreckage at St Cuthman's Church, Whitehawk.

10

THE LAST ATTACKS

MONDAY AUGUST 16 1943

AFTER a hit and run at eighteen minutes after midnight one of a number of German aircraft flew seawards where it was caught for a few seconds in searchlights. Ground defences opened up and minutes later distress flares were seen and the plane fell into the sea.

The downed plane had dropped three bombs on Whitehawk; one landed on the playing fields in Whitehawk Road, a second fell on open ground to the east of Wilson Avenue and the third struck St Cuthman's Church on the corner of Lintott Avenue and Fletching Road. It destroyed the church's organ and the roof and two outer

William Hayler, left, was killed while writing
up his report sheet during the raid. Later the
Brighton ARP gave a concert to raise money
for his family. *Photo: Mrs Peggy Lower*

walls of the modern church collapsed, leaving only the tower standing.

In the church hall, which doubled as a wardens' post, warden William Hayler died as he was writing on his report sheet the time of the raid. A scattered pack of playing cards, a dust covered miniature billiards table and some torn periodicals among a pile of rubble were all that remained of the wardens' half of the hall; strangely the other part was not badly damaged.

Mr Hayler, who worked at Allen West, was a keen allotment gardener and after his death another warden, a Mr Newman, and a friend, carried on with the gardening and sold the produce to raise money for Mr Hayler's widow. Later the wardens put on a concert to raise money for the family.

Nearby a Mrs Cole, her seven year old son Raymond and her mother, Mrs Weller, had a narrow escape; they had left a bedroom for the Morrison table shelter and when they returned to the bedroom after the raid they found a block of masonry had crashed through the wall leaving a gaping hole several feet wide at the back of the bed.

FRIDAY OCTOBER 22 1943
IN the early hours of this autumn Friday a lone German aircraft dived from the clouds, the screaming of its engine alerting people, giving

them precious minutes to scramble for their shelters. It is thought the target was the railway viaduct again, part of which crosses Lewes Road near the junction with Upper Lewes Road.

A 500kg bomb was released but it fell short and landed on the railway track in the cutting next to Bonchurch Street. It exploded on impact behind No. 79. There were no deaths but eleven people needed to

The smashed railway line in the cutting behind Bonchurch Street.

be treated for their injuries. Three of them were taken to hospital. Houses nearest to the impact suffered from the blast and a number or roofs collapsed, covering those still in their beds with dust and debris.

Almost all of the windows of Elm Grove School were smashed or blown out and the Sunny Bank Laundry at 82–84 Bonchurch Street was all but demolished.

Houses in Seville Street and Wellington Street were also affected, with smashed windows and broken roof tilesand slates. One of the residents said that the whole house seemed to sway backwards and forwards, and in another house a piano was lifted up and hurled across the room.

The bomb fell at 3.45am and the blast was likened by Mrs Bower, who lived near the laundry, to an earthquake.

Despite the hour, the rescue services arrived within minutes and they and neighbours set about helping the injured. A welfare centre was set up and those familes made temporarily homeless went there for food and rest.

WEDNESDAY FEBRUARY 23 1944

EAST Brighton was again the target on this cold night when a number of high explosive bombs were dropped. Just before they were released a German plane was trapped in searchlight beams and it may have jettisoned the bombs in an effort to escape.

The worst hit streets included Bennett Road, Rugby Place and Eastern Road; Marine Gate was hit yet again, as was Wilsons Laundry in Arundel Road.

Eleven people died that night. One was Alfred Saunders, stepson of Henry Holden who had fought with General Custer at the Battle of the Little Bighorn in 1876. Alfred was found dead in the garden of his home in Bennett Road.

This was the third time that the area had been bombed, and again, extensive damage was caused to many houses. The Morrison shelter saved the lives of the Burnett family of four whose house tumbled down around them, but they escaped without a scratch. And another family who owed their lives to the shelter were the Dinnages whose house was also demolished.

Wilsons Laundry in Arundel Road. *Photo: Brighton Reference Library.*

Part of the laundry was damaged, including the staff canteen, and a gas main in Arundel Road was fractured and caught fire. By 8am the following morning repairs had already been started on the damaged houses and an information office was set up to help those whose property and houses had been damaged or lost.

KILLED AS A RESULT OF ENEMY ACTION ON WEDNESDAY FEBRUARY 23 1944

BEADLE George, 55,
19 Rugby Place.
BRADSTOCK Rosina, 60,
68 Bennett Road.
MORLEY Harry, 39,
35 Bennett Road.
MORLEY John Mervin,
35 Bennett Road, at RSCH the next day.
READING Alfred, 56,
44 Bennett Road.
SAUNDERS Alfred, 61,

41 Bennett Road.
SHERLOCK Edith, 62,
24 Bennett Road.
SHERLOCK William, 63
24 Bennett Road.
WEAVER Edith Lucy 70,
49 Bennett Road.
WEAVER Joseph Reginald, 44,
49 Bennett Road.
WILLIAMS Doris Caroline, 23,
246 Eastern Road.

TUESDAY MARCH 14 1944

A FEW minutes after 1am a low flying aircraft was heard almost at the same time as were three clear and distinct explosions. The bombs landed in the sea a few hundred yards from the shore line.

Blast damage was caused to windows and roofs on the seafront, including the Metropole Hotel, and shops and businesses in Western Road also suffered, but no injuries were reported.

WEDNESDAY MARCH 22 1944

A BOMB from a high flying aircraft was dropped on Old Farm Road, Patcham, at 1.09am, causing substantial damage to Nos. 5 and 6 and scattering tiles on neighbouring houses.

A twenty one feet crater was made in the road and the gas main was fractured – but there was no fire. Also fractured was the nine inch sewer. Two heavy manhole covers were lifted by the blast and hurled several feet. There were no casualties.

THE END OF THE WAR IN EUROPE

FRIDAY MAY 8 1945

AS the war in Europe came to an end the celebrations started. Almost every street in Brighton had a street party in May, 1945. This photograph from the author's collection shows the children of Grove Street, and their parents. David Rowland, then ten years old, is pictured third row in just to the right of the downpipe in the second entrance from the left. He is the lad in the white, open necked shirt standing between two women. His grandmother is standing in the pavement with his cousin, Derek, who is holding the Union flag.

CRASHED AIRCRAFT

THURSDAY SEPTEMBER 19 1940

A JUNKERS 88 from 3 Staffel Kampfgeschwader 51 crashed into the English Channel and sank off the Sussex coast – cause unknown. The crew of four were Oberfeldwebel Luckard, Unteroffizier Henker, Feldwebel Walter and Gefreiter Roeder.

On November 4 the body of Unteroffizier Waldemar Henker, twenty two years old, was washed ashore at Brighton. He was buried in the cemetery in Bear Road.

WEDNESDAY APRIL 30 1941

LAWRENCE HOLFORD, a forty eight year old war reserve police constable, was on patrol in the Lewes Road area. His route covered Dewe Road, where the Allen West factory was engaged in war work.

At about 3pm PC Holford called in on the gatekeeper, Stephen Dyer; both were in the gatekeeper's hut when disaster struck. There had been a number of allied aircraft in the sky above Brighton. Suddenly two Beaufighters collided; there was a deafening crash and the planes disintegrated over the factory. The engine of one smashed down through the hut, killing PC Holford and Mr Dyer instantly. The other engine fell on allotments in Roedale Road.

The Beaufighter, then, was still on the secret list, and local reports of the tragedy referred to the downed planes as Spitfires.

Such was the impact that pieces of the doomed aircraft were scattered over a large area of the town. Bill Cowan, a twenty one year old police constable, was having an afternoon sleep, after an early shift, in his digs in Edburton Avenue, when he was woken by the sound of heavy items falling in the street. Rushing outside he saw parts of aircraft and the debris from shattered roofs.

Another policeman, Dennis Hines, reported finding a large piece of one of the Beaufighters on waste ground at the south end of Roedale Road opposite what was then the Palmerston Laundry. Minor damage was caused to the garden wall of the first house, occupied by the local coalman, Mr Church.

One pilot managed to parachute to safety but the three other aircrew of the two planes were killed – one crashing through the roof of a house in Roedale Road.

At the inquest, the coroner, Charles Webb, recorded a verdict of accidental death on Mr Dyer, of 3 Redvers Road, and PC Holford, who had lived at 19 Ditchling Road.

SUNDAY JUNE 1 1941

THE licensee of the pub at Poynings, on Brighton's northern boundary, had just gone to bed on the night of Sunday, June 1, 1941, when he and his wife heard the roar of a low flying plane. It was obvious the aircraft was in trouble. Within a few seconds there was a tremendous crash and the blazing aircraft lit up the night sky.

It was a Junkers 88, A5 (No 6325) and it had come down at Poynings Spring, Saddlescombe, close to the Devil's Dyke. The landlord and a number of soldiers rushed to the scene where they saw something white waving in the moonlight, and heard a voice calling 'Kamerad'. They found a young German officer, injured and entangled in his parachute. He had a bullet wound in his foot. Then a second German was discovered, uninjured, wandering near the wrecked plane.

Both were arrested and handed over to the police. The injured airman, Feldwebel Stein, was treated at the Royal Sussex County Hospital and he and Feldwebel H Riedel were then taken to a prisoner of war camp.

Gefreiter A Rosenhahn was burned to death in the crash and a search of the area found the fourth member of the crew, Feldwebel K Ilsemann, dead with a broken neck in a nearby wood. His parachute had failed to open. He was wearing the Iron Cross on his uniform.

The Junkers was one of 110 aircraft that had raided Manchester that night, and was the only one lost. It had been shot down shortly before midnight by Wing Commander Allen in a Beaufighter of 219 Squadron, Tangmere.

Throughout Whit Monday the wrecked plane attracted large numbers of sightseers.

THURSDAY MAY 8 1942

AT 2.59am a Heinkel 111 from Kampfgeschwader 100 pathfinder unit crashed at Ewebottom, Patcham.

It had crossed the eastern edge of Brighton at a height of 7,000 feet and travelled three miles inland when it was spotted by a Bristol Beaufighter from 219 Squadron at Tangmere, crewed by Squadron Leader JG Topham and Flying Officer HW Berridge. The Heinkel was hit in the first burst of cannon fire and as it started to go down three bombs fell.

The aircraft struck power cables in a field 600 yards east of the A23 and exploded with such force that pieces were found scattered over a very wide area, including Sweet Hill on the other side of the railway line. One part of the wreckage was found on the sports field at Patcham and most of the other pieces landed on farm land north of the Black Lion pub.

A 1,000kg bomb landed in the back garden of 20 Highview Avenue but failed to explode. It made a crater twenty six feet deep and threw a quantity of chalk some fifty feet. Miraculously the house was not damaged.

A smaller 250kg bomb also failed to explode and was found about 250 yards north west of the crashed aircraft, making a crater seventeen feet deep. The third bomb, also 250kg, blew up close to the wreckage.

All five of the crew were killed. One had bailed out but his parachute failed to open. Two were wearing the Iron Cross. They were buried with full military honours at the Bear Road cemetery.

THURSDAY AUGUST 19 1942

A JUNKERS 88 from 3 Kustenfliegergruppe 106 was shot down by Sergeant Clee and Sergeant Grant flying a Beaufighter of 141 Squadron. The time was 6.15pm and the enemy aircraft crashed into the sea four miles off Selsey Bill.

The crew were Gefreiter F Heidsiek, Unteroffizier F Nottmeier, Gefreiter H Zur Nieden and Gefreiter W Bleiber. The body of twenty year old Bleiber was washed ashore on Saturday, September 5, near the Highcliffe Cafe at Rottingdean. He was buried with military honours at the Bear Road cemetery.

The four crew of the crashed Dornier were buried with full military honours at Bear Road cemetery on February 20, 1943.

THURSDAY FEBRUARY 10 1943

TAKING advantage of low cloud, a number of German fighters and fighter- bombers machine gunned Brighton's streets in the middle of the afternoon.

A Dornier 217 of 5 Staffel Kampfgschwader 40, coming from the south west, was flying low over open ground behind the Butlins hotel at Saltdean when it encountered heavy anti aircraft fire. The plane was hit and it crashed on open ground north of Homebush Avenue, exploding into small pieces. A headless body was found outside the front door of 18 Homebush Avenue.

The crew were Obergefreiter Emil Jakubassa, twenty three; Unteroffizier Franz Kusters, twenty; Oberfeldwebel Otto Schneider, twenty nine; Feldwebel Herbert Teichgraber, twenty five. All were buried with military honours in the Bear Road cemetery.

FRIDAY MARCH 24 1944

A JUNKERS 88 from 6 Staffel Kampfgeschwader 6 was shot down at 11.53pm by a Mosquito of 465 Squadron crewed by Wing

Commander K M Hampshire and Flying Officer T Condon.

The Junkers crashed at Walberton, near Arundel. The crew baled out but two died when their parachutes failed to open, one landed in the sea and was drowned and the fourth was captured alive, but injured. The body of the drowned German came ashore at Black Rock in Brighton on Wednesday, May 3, and he was buried in the Bear Road cemetery.

TUESDAY APRIL 19 1944

THE last attack of the Baby Blitz, a renewed offensive against London in the spring of 1944, occurred on this particular night. Taking part was twenty four year old Oberleutnant Richard Pahl in a Messerschmitt 410A–1 (no.420293) of 1 Staffel Kampfgeschwader 51 based at Evreux in France. Pahl's wireless operator was Feldwebel Wilhelm Schuberth.

The Messerschmitt, damaged by flak over London, was first seen north of Brighton that night heading for home across the Channel. It was spotted by the crew of a Mosquito of 96 Squadron, from West Malling in Kent, crewed by Wing Commander ED Crew and Warrant Officer Croysdill.

A close up of the Messerschmitt tailplane among the graves in St Nicholas churchyard.

The time was 12.48am. The Mosquito opened fire and there was a large flash from the raider, followed by sheets of flame. The Messerschmitt turned towards Brighton, losing height. Schuberth baled out and was drowned in the sea. His body was washed up the next day near Friston and he was buried in the local churchyard (and later moved to the military cemetery at Cannock Chase).

The Messerschmitt crashed on to the lower part of Dyke Road, striking a lamp standard and ploughing into the flint wall of St Nicholas's churchyard. It was blazing fiercely, fuelled by igniting flares, and there was great danger of ammunition and bombs still in the aircraft exploding.

The tail and parts of the fuselage fell among tombstones and many of the graves were disturbed and had their headstones broken or knocked down. Eventually the plane burnt itself out.

The pilot was found dead, hanging by his parachute cords from a tree on the opposite side of the road. He had a shrapnel wound on his head.

Eileen Donoghue, then living at 5 Dyke Road, had gone out on the town with her brother and sister in law for the first time since the start of the war. She returned late and had just gone to bed when she felt something heavy crash on to the bed beside her. She could see there was a fire outside close by. She got up and rushed outside where she saw a German airman hanging in a tree; he appeared to be on fire. Later she found that the object that landed on her bed was part of the churchyard wall.

Pahl was a much decorated officer, who had been wounded three times. He had been awarded the Iron Cross which he was wearing when he died. He was buried in the Bear Road cemetery.

AIR RAID PRECAUTIONS

BEFORE the war began the Home Office issued every householder with a little booklet entitled *The Protection of your Home Against Air Raids.* This explained about the importance of the blackout – the darkening of every window, skylight or glass door with thick curtains or blinds so that enemy aircraft should not see any lights at night; and described how to create a refuge room.

The best place for a refuge room was a cellar or basement. It was a place easy to reach, and to get out of, where people could be reasonably safe during an air raid. They were advised to stock it with candles and matches, an electric hand lamp, tins and jars of food, drinking water, chamber pots and toilet paper (with a screen for privacy), a bottle of disinfectant, first aid supplies, books, toys for the children, spare blankets and mattresses and a wireless set.

The refuge room had to be sealed against the entry of gas, and the way to do it was to fill in all cracks and crevices with putty or a pulp made from sodden newspaper. Cracks in walls and ceiling had to be papered over, and cracks in the floorboards also needed to be filled. Ventilators had to be stopped up with rags or pasted over with thick paper. Windows also had to be sealed and wedged firmly in their frames, and the panes covered with thick brown paper.

All doors which need not be used had to be sealed, and the remaining door had to have, on the outside, a blanket fixed securely to the frame with just a flap to go in and out of the room. If the blanket were kept damp during the air raid it gave better protection. For extra safety, wooden props could be fixed to support the ceiling

In a sealed refuge room ten feet by ten feet five people could remain in complete safety for twelve hours, without ventilation, the booklet said. The arrival of Anderson and Morrison shelters later lessened the need for refuge rooms. The booklet also advised householders to clear the loft, attic or top floor of all inflammable material and to protect the floor with sheets of corrugated iron, sheet iron or asbestos wallboard, or failing that with two inches of sand.

THE EFFECTS OF A BOMB EXPLOSION

THIS is the account of a man who experienced a massive bomb explosion near at hand, remained conscious and survived to tell the tale.

'The explosion made an indescribable noise – something like a colossal growl – and was accompanied by a veritable tornado of air blast. I felt an excruciating pain in my ears and all sounds were replaced by a very loud singing noise, which I was told later was when I lost my hearing and had my eardrums perforated.

'I felt that consciousness was slipping from me. . . and summoning all my willpower and energy, I succeeded in forcing myself down into a crouching position with my knees on the ground, my feet against the kerb behind me and my hands covering my face. I remember having to move them over my ears because of the pain in them. It seemed to ease the pain. Then I received another hit on the forehead and felt weaker. The blast seemed to come in successive waves accompanied by vibrations from the ground. I felt as if it were trying to spin me and tear me away from the kerb.

'Then I received a very heavy blow just in front of the right temple, which knocked me down on my left side in the gutter. Later, in the first aid post, they removed what they described as a piece of bomb from that wound. Whilst in the gutter I clung on to the kerb with both hands and with my feet against it. I was again hit in the right chest, and later found that my double breasted overcoat, my coat, leather comb case and papers had been cut clean through and a watch in the top right hand pocket of my waistcoat had the back dented in and its works broken.

'Just as I felt that I could not hold out much longer I realised that the blast pressure was decreasing and a shower of dust, dirt and rubble swept across me. Pieces penetrated my face, some skin was blown off, something pierced my left thumbnail and my knuckles were cut, causing me involuntarily to let go my hold on the kerb. Instantly, although the blast was dying down, I felt myself being slowly blown across the pavement towards the wall of a building. I tried to hold on, but there was nothing to hold on to. Twice I tried to rise, but seemed held down; eventually I staggered to my feet. . . I wondered where the water was coming from, which I felt dripping down my face, and quickly discovered that it was blood from my head wounds.'

This account comes from *Front Line 1940–1941*, the official story of the Civil Defence, issued for the Ministry of Home Security by the Ministry of Information, published by HMSO, 1942.

GERMAN AIRCRAFT

THE **JUNKERS 88** was built as a Schnellbomber, a medium sized bomber but with the speed of a fighter. It was possibly the most successful German aircraft ever built.

The JU 88 was extremely adaptable and fulfilled the roles of night bomber, night fighter, intruder, reconnaissance plane, heavy day bomber, torpedo bomber and anti-tank aircraft.

It had two engines, each of 1,400hp, a wing span of about sixty six feet and a length of forty seven feet. It carried a crew of four and had a maximum speed of 273mph. The maximum range of the aircraft was 1,500 miles.

The **Heinkel 111** was the largest of the German bombers to fly over England and at the time was probably the most famous. It had two engines, a wing span of seventy four feet and a length of fifty four feet six inches. The aircraft carried a crew of five, had a maximum speed of 258mph and a range of 1,100 miles. It was armed with a cannon and six machine guns, plus a bomb load of some 10,000kg.

The Heinkel 111 was also used with great success as a torpedo bomber and, most spectacularly, as a missile launch pad, with flying bombs being launched at night over the North Sea, destined for London.

The **Messerschmitt 109** was a single seater fighter that first saw combat duty in the Spanish Civil War. Several models were produced, each time with an increase in engine power.

The 109 E single engine fighter, involved in the Battle of Britain, easily bettered the Hurricane, but it met its match with the Spitfire. The limited range of the 109E allowed only a few minutes' combat time over southern England. It had a wing span of a little over thirty two feet and a length of just under twenty nine feet. Maximum speed was 354mph and maximum range just 412 miles. The aircraft was equipped with two 7.09mm machine guns and three 20mm cannons.

The 109 F appeared during 1941. It has an uprated 1,300hp engine, maximum speed of 373mph and was about the same size. It carried one 15mm MG 151 cannon and two 7.0mm MG 17 machine guns.

By the end of 1941 the 109 G had replaced almost all of the previous models and accounted for some seventy per cent of the total 109 production. The single DB 605 engine was capable of 1,450hp with a range of 350 miles, and it had three cannons and two machine guns.

The **Dornier 217** entered service early in 1941. A total of 1,730 had been built when production ended two years later. This aircraft played a prominent role in the Baedecker raids of 1942, when very serious damaged was caused at night to British cities.

It was a large aircraft, used mainly as a night bomber. There were two 1,750hp DB 603 A engines, and the Dornier had a wingspan of sixty two feet and a length of a little under fifty six feet. It carried a crew of four, had a maximum speed of 348mph and a maximum range of 1,550 miles. It was fitted with machine guns and 20mm cannon and the maximum bomb load was 8,820kg.

ABOUT THE AUTHOR

DAVID ROWLAND was four when war broke out on September 3, 1939. He still has vivid memories of the nights when Brighton burned, of sleeping in a Morrison shelter, of carrying a gas mask, and of the many evacuations from the classroom to the surface air raid shelters outside his school.

David's mother died three weeks after he was born and he was adopted by her sister, Edith, and her husband, Charles. In the month the war began his adoptive mother, Edith, died and he went to live with his adoptive father and grandmother at 25a Grove Street, where he remained throughout the war years.

David attended Finsbury Road Junior School and Fawcett School in Pelham Street, and his first job was with Sainsbury, where he stayed for eight years, leaving to join Brighton Borough Police. His twenty seven years' service in Brighton included periods as a dog handler and a patrol car driver. Since 1985 he has been employed by Brighton Co-op, and, latterly, Asda at Brighton Marina.